What's In <u>Your</u> Future?

The Book of Revelation in Chronological Order

Jim Biscardi, Jr. and
Joe Velez

What's In __Your__ Future?
The Book of Revelation in Chronological Order

© 2005 by James Biscardi, Jr.

ISBN 0-9753786-2-7

All Rights Reserved

This document may not be reproduced or transmitted in any form or by any means, electrical, mechanical including photocopying, recording, or any information storage and retrieval system without permission in writing from the publisher.

Published By

Mantle Ministries
PO Box 248
Lanoka Harbor, NJ 08734

Cover design by Faithlyn Robinson
Cover photo by Digitalvision

TABLE OF CONTENTS

Introduction	5
Chapter 1 - Chronology of Events	7
Chapter 2 – Christ Reveals Himself to the Apostle John	11
Chapter 3 – Christ's Warning to the Seven Churches	15
Chapter 4 – Satan Cast to Earth & Unrestrained Lawlessness	35
Chapter 5 – The Rapture of the Church	39
Chapter 6 - The Judgment Seat of Christ	45
Chapter 7 – The Rise of the Antichrist World Ruler and His Prophet	53
Chapter 8 – Technology and the Rise of the Antichrist	59
Chapter 9 – The Marriage Supper of the Lamb	73
Chapter 10 – God's Final Campaign to Save Souls and Recover the Earth	77
Chapter 11 – The Seals and the Angel Messengers	83
Chapter 12 – The Trumpets and the Vials	99
Chapter 13 – The Battle of Armageddon	119
Chapter 14 – Ruling and Reigning With Christ 1000 Years	127
Chapter 15 – New Heaven, New Earth, and New Jerusalem	137

Chapter 16 – Christ's Final Word 145

Epilogue – What The World Could Be Or Will Be in 2030 151

Appendix A – Illustrations 155

Appendix B – Babylon and Continuous Spiritual Warfare 161

Topical Index 167

Cross-Reference Index 171

INTRODUCTION

Everyone wonders about what will be in their future. Our Lord Jesus Christ gave us the answer about 2000 years ago. He commanded the Apostle John to *"write the things which thou hast seen, and the things which are, and the things which shall be hereafter…"* Revelation 1:19. But what John wrote has been a mystery and difficult to decipher even for the most serious and sincere Christian. It requires unraveling many symbols, visions, and above all putting events in their proper sequence.

The Lord is a Rewarder of those who diligently seek Him, and so this Revelation comes with a blessing: *"Blessed is he that readeth, and they that keepeth the words of this prophecy, and keep those things which are written therein: for the time is at hand."* Revelation 1:3.

Though the central person in every book of the Bible is Christ, nowhere is this more apparent than in the Book of Revelation. It is filled with His person, grace, and power. As the Lamb of God, He demonstrates His desire that none should perish – leaving a powerful witness for those left behind after the rapture. As the Head of the Church, He provides both a warning to stay ready for His return, and encouragement that by His strength we can overcome all things. As the returning Messiah, He vanquishes all evil, and claims His right to rule over heaven and earth.

What's In Your Future? is written after studying the Revelation of Jesus Christ for 30 years. We offer a suggested sequence that places events in chronological order, and that also groups symbols together that are reiterating and adding detail to similar events – thus reducing or eliminating repetition. This results in portions of the Book of Revelation being read "out of order." For example, Satan being cast out of heaven and the appearance of the Antichrist (Revelation 12 and 13) appear before the Lamb opens the seven seals (Revelation 6-8).

6 – What's in <u>Your</u> Future?

Our belief is that Revelation is a microcosm of the entire Word of God – where prophecies do not occur in a chronological sequence. For example, the prophecy about Jesus' time of birth (Daniel 9:25) comes from Daniel and His flight into Egypt (Hosea 11:1) comes from Hosea. But chronologically, Hosea preceded Daniel. There are many other examples of this throughout Scripture. For example, Christ's triumphal entry into Jerusalem (Zechariah 9:9) comes from Zechariah. His suffering on the cross for the transgressions of the world (Isaiah 53: 4-5) comes by Isaiah. But chronologically Isaiah precedes Zechariah.

We also gather together scriptures from other <u>parts of God's Word that confirm and add meaning and understanding</u> to the various parts of Revelation. Finally, we have <u>added author insights</u> that will bring perspective and also (we trust) glorify the One and only One who is *"...worthy to receive glory, honor, and power: for (He) ...created all things and for (His) pleasure they are and were created."* Revelation 4: 11.

CHAPTER 1
THE CHRONOLOGY OF EVENTS

- ❖ Persecution of the Church – John exiled to Patmos
- ❖ Christ Reveals Himself to John
- ❖ Christ Warns and Challenges the Seven Churches
- ❖ Satan Cast Down to Earth & Unrestrained Lawlessness
- ❖ The Rapture of the Church (Simultaneous with Satan cast down)
- ❖ The Judgment Seat of Christ – The Bride of Christ makes herself ready (In heaven while other events take place on earth)
- ❖ Rise of the Antichrist and False Prophet
  - o Amplifying Scriptures
    - Daniel 9:27 – False peace treaty with Israel broken after 3 ½ years
    - Daniel 11:37 – Puts himself above everything and everyone
    - Revelation 13: 2,7 – Receives power and authority over the nations from Satan
    - Revelation 6: 9-11, 7: 9-17 – Kills millions of believers
    - Revelation 19: 20 – A false prophet serves the Antichrist and demands his image be worshipped (Revelation 13:14)
- ❖ The Marriage Supper of the Lamb (In heaven while other events take place on earth) – The saints are dressed for the battle of righteousness.
- ❖ God's Campaign to Save Souls Left Behind and Recover the Earth
  - o First Seal & Angel Messenger – The gospel is preached by God's special witnesses
  - o Second Seal & Angel Messenger – The gospel brings division and takes peace from the earth. The Lord commands His people to come out of "Babylon" before her destruction.

- Third Seal & Angel Messenger – God's Judgment on those who take the mark of the Beast – a high price for physical survival.
    - Fourth Seal & Angel Messenger – Many refuse the mark. They accept Christ and give up their lives – Death is a blessing.
    - Fifth Seal & Angel Messenger – Christ "reaps the earth" of those who are His.
    - Sixth Seal & Angel Messenger – Unbelievers are "reaped" and thrown into the winepress of God's wrath. God's remnant of Jews, (i.e.144,000 in number) are sealed for protection from God's wrath. Believers who come out of great tribulation report for duty as they stand before God's throne.
    - Seventh Seal & Angel Messenger – Angels get ready to execute God's wrath.
- ❖ God's Wrath Executed by Seven Trumpets and Seven Vials. It serves two purposes: Punishment of the nations and restoring Israel to spiritual favor. It's the time of Jacob's Trouble (Jeremiah 30:7). 2/3 of Jews on earth die. See Zechariah 13: 8-9 and Ezekiel 36: 24-28.
    - Wrath against the earth
    - Wrath against the sea
    - Wrath against the rivers and fountains of waters
    - Wrath against the sun
    - Wrath against man through locusts from the bottomless pit
    - Wrath against the River Euphrates.
        - God gives John a prophetic ministry to tell what he's seen
        - Mystery Babylon is exposed and her destruction prophesied. God's last call for His people to leave her before she is destroyed.
    - Wrath against man from the plague of hail
- ❖ Christ Returns with His Saints to win the Battle of Armageddon
    - Amplifying Scriptures

- Daniel 11:44 – Antichrist is opposed from North and East
- Revelation 16:12-16 – Final showdown in the plains of Megiddo
- Zechariah 14: 1-2 – The fighting will reach Jerusalem and the Jews suffer horribly
- Zechariah 14: 3-9 – When all seems hopeless, Christ with His saints descend to the Mount of Olives (Revelation 19: 11-21). The mountain splits and forms a new valley from Jordan to the Mediterranean Sea (Zechariah 14: 3-9). And the Jews are strengthened (Zechariah 12: 6-9)
- Zechariah 14, 12,15, - God sends a plague on His enemies and animals

❖ Christ Rules and Reigns With His Saints on Earth
  o Amplifying Scriptures
    - Matthew 25: 31-46 – Jesus separates the goats and the sheep.
    - Revelation 20: 4-6 - Christ rules the earth with His saints
    - Jeremiah 23:5 - Christ will be King
    - Isaiah 2: 1-3 - Israel will be prominent
    - Christ's rule will reflect His character: Justice - Isaiah 2:4, All prosper – Micah 4: 1-4, Righteousness – Jeremiah 23:5, Peace – Zechariah 8: 4-5, People safe – Jeremiah 23: 4-5
    - The natural world is transformed: Climate – Isaiah 30: 23-26, Animals tame – Isaiah 11: 6-8, Fishing is great – Ezekiel 47: 9-10, Life lengthened – Isaiah 65: 19-20,22, Trees provide food and medicine – Ezekiel 47: 12
    - Malachi 1:11 – God's name known in all the world
    - Zechariah 14:16 – Everyone from all nations come to see Christ

❖ The Last Rebellion

10 – What's In <u>Your</u> Future?
- ❖ The White Throne Judgment
- ❖ New Heaven, New Earth, and New Jerusalem

CHAPTER 2
JESUS REVEALS HIMSELF TO THE APOSTLE JOHN

Jesus is the Revealer of Revelation; the Beginning and Ending of the Christian life; the Judge of believers, churches, and unbelievers; the Commander-in-Chief of the spiritual and physical battles of Revelation; the Reason for the struggles of Revelation; the King-of-kings; the Light of the New Jerusalem; and, the Architect of the new heaven and new earth.

John calls Him the One who is, and who was, and who is to come (Revelation 1:4). Jesus, Himself, adds "the Alpha and Omega" and "the Almighty" (Revelation 1:8) and "the First and the Last." (Revelation 1:17). He has no beginning and has no end. He is ever-present and all-powerful. Before ascending to sit at the right hand of the Father, Jesus said, *"All authority in heaven and on earth has been given to me."* Matthew 28:18. He is the One coming back – for His people and for the kingdom of the world (Revelation 11:15).

He is the "I AM" who spoke to Moses out of the burning bush. Exodus 3:14. After referring to Himself as the "I AM" in that verse, Jesus then said, *"Say to the Israelites, 'The Lord, the God of your fathers – the God of Abraham, the God of Isaac, the God of Jacob – has sent me to you. This is my name forever, the name by which I am to be remembered from generation to generation.'"* Exodus 3:15. The Hebrew for "Lord" in this verse sounds like and may be derived from the Hebrew for "I AM." Remember, Jesus told the Jews who questioned Him, *"I tell you the truth, before Abraham was born, I AM!"* See John 8:58.

Jesus had already revealed Himself to John as the "I AM… the Messiah (John 4:26); the Bread of Life (John 6:35); the Eternal One (John 8:58); the Light of the World (John 9:5); the Door (John 10:7); the Son of God (John 10:36); the Resurrection and the Life

(John 11:25); the Lord and Master (John 13:13); The Way, the Truth, and the Life (John 14:6); and, the True Vine (John 15:1).

John calls Him the faithful witness, firstborn from the dead, and the ruler of the kings of the earth (Revelation 1:5). Jesus adds that He was dead but is the Living One who is alive forever, and holds the keys to death and Hades (Revelation 1:18). Christ proved Himself to be faithful as the Lamb of God, dying for the sins of the world. All who receive Him receive life. Those who do not will be condemned to death. He also proved faithful in resurrection! He said, *"I am the resurrection and the life. He who believes in me will live, even though he dies; and whoever lives and believes in me will never die."* John 11:25, 26.

Revelation 1: 1-18[1]

¹ The Revelation of Jesus Christ, which God gave Him to show His servants--things which must shortly take place. And He sent and signified it by His angel to His servant John, ²who bore witness to the word of God, and to the testimony of Jesus Christ, to all things that he saw. ³Blessed is he who reads and those who hear the words of this prophecy, and keep those things which are written in it; for the time is near.

⁴John, to the seven churches which are in Asia: Grace to you and peace from Him who is and who was and who is to come, and from the seven Spirits who are before His throne, ⁵and from Jesus Christ, the faithful witness, the firstborn from the dead, and the ruler over the kings of the earth. To Him who loved us and washed us from our sins in His own blood, ⁶and has made us kings and priests to His God and Father, to Him be glory and dominion forever and ever. Amen.

⁷Behold, He is coming with clouds, and every eye will see Him, even they who pierced Him. And all the tribes of the earth will mourn because of Him. Even so, Amen. ⁸"I am the Alpha and the

---

[1] The text of the Book of Revelation is the New King James Version

Omega, the Beginning and the End, "says the Lord, "who is and who was and who is to come, the Almighty."

⁹I, John, both your brother and companion in the tribulation and kingdom and patience of Jesus Christ, was on the island that is called Patmos for the word of God and for the testimony of Jesus Christ. ¹⁰I was in the Spirit on the Lord's Day, and I heard behind me a loud voice, as of a trumpet, ¹¹saying, "I am the Alpha and the Omega, the First and the Last," and, "What you see, write in a book and send it to the seven churches which are in Asia: to Ephesus, to Smyrna, to Pergamos, to Thyatira, to Sardis, to Philadelphia, and to Laodicea."

¹²Then I turned to see the voice that spoke with me. And having turned I saw seven golden lampstands, ¹³and in the midst of the seven lampstands One like the Son of Man, clothed with a garment down to the feet and girded about the chest with a golden band. ¹⁴His head and hair were white like wool, as white as snow, and His eyes like a flame of fire; ¹⁵His feet were like fine brass, as if refined in a furnace, and His voice as the sound of many waters; ¹⁶He had in His right hand seven stars, out of His mouth went a sharp two-edged sword, and His countenance was like the sun shining in its strength. ¹⁷And when I saw Him, I fell at His feet as dead. But He laid His right hand on me, saying to me, "Do not be afraid; I am the First and the Last. ¹⁸I am He who lives, and was dead, and behold, I am alive forevermore. Amen. And I have the keys of Hades and of Death.

Help us, O Lord, to live our lives
So people clearly see
Reflections of Your caring heart,
Your love and purity.
— *Sper*

CHAPTER 3
CHRIST'S WARNING TO THE SEVEN CHURCHES

The Book of Revelation was written for the seven churches – representative of all God's people. Jesus told John, *"What thou seest write in a book and send it unto the seven churches which are in Asia…"* Revelation 1:11.

As the Righteous Judge of Revelation, Jesus will preside at the White Throne judgment of unbelievers. Revelation 20:11-15. He is also the Judge of believers at the Judgment Seat of Christ. 2 Corinthians 5:10. In the scenes that follow, we see Christ, as Revealer and Righteous Judge demonstrating His grace and the sternness of His love. He's warning us all – through these seven representative churches - to get ready for His return and His judgment of us.

Before His crucifixion, Jesus prayed to His Father about all His disciples (i.e. the Church), *"That they all may be one; as thou, Father, art in me, and I in thee, that they also may be one in us: that the world may believe that thou hast sent me."* John 17:21. It is eternally important that all Christians - the Body of Christ – the Church – the kingdom of God - maintain the unity of the Spirit in the bond of peace (Ephesians 4: 3). Because by reflecting the

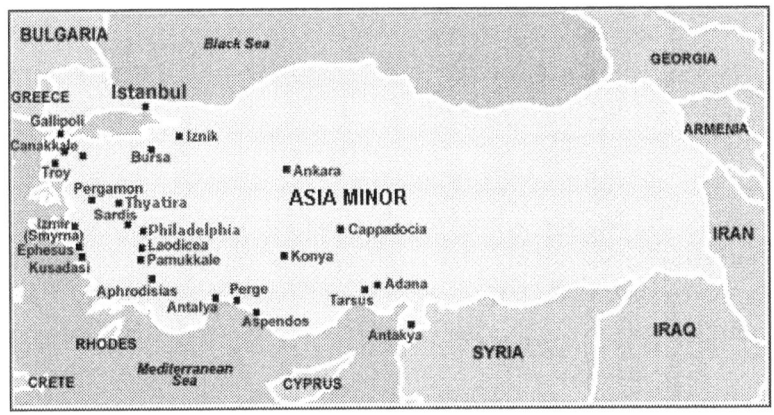

image of Christ to the whole watching world, people would believe that God sent Christ - and accept Him.

Because it is so important that the Church emulate Christ, the Revealer and Righteous Judge provided feedback to the seven churches (Revelation 2 and 3) to expose their sin, lead them to repent, and help them mature in His ways and purposes. These churches, though physically in the area now known as Turkey, were to be representative of all churches and also representative of issues that individual Christians face.

We must remember that there are two kingdoms of God – a visible and invisible one. The kingdom of God is the spiritual rule of God in the hearts of His people through Jesus Christ. The visible one is called the Church, made up of all those who accept Jesus as Savior and follow Him as Lord. The invisible one is the one within each believer. In Luke 17: 20-21 Jesus said, *"The kingdom of God is within you."* Romans 14:17 says that the kingdom of God *" is righteousness, peace, and joy in the Holy Ghost."* God is working in each of those kingdoms. The visible kingdom, however, only grows as the invisible one in each believer grows and produces the fruit of the Spirit (Galatians 5: 22-26) and the character of Christ (Philippians 2: 5-11).

These seven churches were also to be representative of different future periods for the Church – from its beginning to the end of the Church era. See Appendix A.

Ephesus had become so active – working in its own strength rather than in the power of the Holy Spirit - that it lost its First Love. **Smyrna** thought it was poor because it didn't have many material possessions – but it was really rich with the gold that comes from having their faith tried in the fire of affliction. (1 Peter 1:7). **Pergamum** was heretical allowing doctrines of devils. Jesus said that He knew where Satan's seat was in that church. **Thyatira** was tolerating a lying prophetess. Not only were they stretching the truth but they also had serious moral and spiritual compromise.

Sardis had a better reputation than they deserved because they were dying spiritually. **Philadelphia** was a loyal church, which had been obedient to God's Word and developed Christ's character. **Laodicea** was lukewarm and self-satisfied.

These same attitudes and behaviors are in the Church today. And, regrettably, they remain *in us* who call ourselves Christians. Our Precious Lord in His grace is warning (and challenging) churches in His visible kingdom, and individuals in the invisible kingdom. He's giving us time to better prepare for His return – to live NOW with a view toward ETERNITY. Jesus had four main messages for those seven churches:

1.   Before He gave each church His judgment about them, He always presented a portrait of Himself that the particular church needed to see. For example, to the Philadelphia church He introduced Himself as, *"...he that is holy, he that is true, he that hath the key of David, he that openeth and no man shutteth; and shutteth and no man openeth..."* He was telling them (and us) to always keep a picture of Him (i.e. who He is) in the center of their hearts and minds.

He revealed Himself to John in chapter 1 with all the attributes of His character that He then divides up and presents to each of the seven churches depending on its need. John prayed that these churches would have peace (1:4). Jesus then gave them the portrait of Himself that would bring peace. *"Thou will keep him in perfect peace, whose mind is stayed on thee: because he trusteth in thee."* Isaiah 26:3.

2.   He told every church that He knew their works. This could be reassuring. But for some of us it should, at times, be disconcerting too! The Lord knows us inside and out. He knows when we hurt one another – how we ambush each other with anger, jealousy, deceit, immorality, slander, lack of forgiveness, pride, stealing, and betrayal.

3. He told four of the seven churches to <u>repent</u>. *"If we confess our sins, he is faithful and just to forgive us our sins, and to cleanse us from all unrighteousness."* (1 John 1:9). We must change the wrong beliefs, attitudes, and behaviors we see in ourselves. We must also take our stand against such things in the Church.

4. He told all the churches to <u>overcome</u>. It's similar to His message to Joshua as he took charge of God's people, *"There shall not any man be able to stand before thee all the days of thy life: as I was with Moses, so I will be with thee; I will not fail thee, nor forsake thee. <u>Be strong and of good courage</u>: for unto this people shalt thou divide for an inheritance the land…Only be thou strong and courageous…Be strong and of good courage; be not afraid, neither be thou dismayed: <u>for the Lord thy God is with thee whithersoever thou goest.</u>"* (Joshua 1: 5-9).

Jesus also told His disciples, *"Never will I leave you; never will I forsake you."* (Hebrews 13:5). We must remember Philippians 4:13, *"I can do everything through him (Christ) who gives me strength."* With the Holy Spirit within to empower each believer, we <u>can in deed</u> overcome - and by unity with our brothers and sisters in Christ, witness to a dying world that Jesus Christ is the only Way to eternal life.

Jesus begins by referring to the "angels of the seven churches. He also refers to the churches themselves as "candlesticks" (KJV) – also translated "lampstands" (NKJV). The Greek word for angel in this context probably refers to the "messenger" or pastor of these churches. He knew how important it was for a church leader to know the truth and to maintain a Christ-believing example for church members.

A lampstand is a fitting symbol for a church. While in this world, Jesus Christ was the light of the world. But He told His disciples, *"You are the light of the world."* Matthew 5:14. Although we give light, we do not originate light. Just as a lampstand gets its light from oil or electricity generating through it, so the child of God is a means of light. Christ is the light, but He uses the church, made up of individual believers, as a lampstand to convey His light. The only limitation placed on the brilliance of the light is the yieldedness of the lampstand.

Revelation 1: 19–20

[19]Write the things which you have seen, and the things which are, and the things which will take place after this. [20]The mystery of the seven stars which you saw in My right hand, and the seven golden lampstands: The seven stars are the angels of the seven churches, and the seven lampstands which you saw are the seven churches.

THE CHURCH AT EPHESUS[2]

Ephesus is considered by bible scholars to have been one of the finest and largest churches of the New Testament times. It was begun by the Apostle Paul at the end of his second missionary journey. Acts 18:19-20. Located in a wicked city given over to the worship of the goddess Artemis, the church exhibited a spiritual vitality that carried over from Paul's habit of preaching "publicly and from house to house," ministering to them "with great humility and with tears" Acts 20:19-20.

Ephesus needs to see Jesus as the one who holds their leader in His right hand and as the One who walks among them. They had exchanged their love of Him for the reward of good deeds. Their obedience was out of ritual – not out of love for Christ. It reminds us of Martha, who was distracted by all the preparations in making Jesus a meal, while her sister Mary stayed at Jesus' feet. Luke 10:38-42. Unless they made a love relationship with Him their priority, which would result in their following Him in their works, He would remove their "lampstand" (i.e. their ability to give light).

---

[2] Excerpts on churches taken from *Revelation Unveiled*, Tim Lahaye, 1999 and *The Second Coming of Christ*, Clarence Larkin, 1918

20 – What's In <u>Your</u> Future?

Revelation 2: 1-7

[1] "To the angel of the church of Ephesus write,

"These things says He who holds the seven stars in His right hand, who walks in the midst of the seven golden lampstands: [2] "I know your works, your labor, your patience, and that you cannot bear those who are evil. And you have tested those who say they are apostles and are not, and have found them liars; [3] and you have persevered and have patience, and have labored for My name's sake and have not become weary. [4] Nevertheless I have this against you, that you have left your first love. [5] Remember therefore from where you have fallen; repent and do the first works, or else I will come to you quickly and remove your lampstand from its place-- unless you repent. [6] But this you have, that you hate the deeds of the Nicolaitans, which I also hate.

[7] "He who has an ear, let him hear what the Spirit says to the churches. To him who overcomes I will give to eat from the tree of life, which is in the midst of the Paradise of God."'

THE CHURCH AT SMYRNA

The church at Smyrna was a much-persecuted church in a wealthy city that had little time for Christians. The Smyrna period of Church history is probably the greatest time of persecution the Church of Christ has ever known. Satan unleashed a violent attack on the Church in an effort to obliterate it, for it became evident to him that the apostolic Church, because of its faithful preaching of the gospel, had become a serious threat to his worldwide godless empire. The more he persecuted the Church during this period, the more the Church overcame the condemning characteristic of the apostolic age - that of having left its first love.

During this time of persecution the emperor of Rome was Diocletian (AD 284-305), who was considered to be the worst Emperor in Rome's history and the greatest antagonist of the

Christian faith. Under his leadership, many cities had public burnings of the Scriptures. Christians were brought to the amphitheater to be fed to the lions while thousands of spectators watched. Many were crucified and others were covered with animal skins and tortured to death by wild dogs. They were covered with tar and set on fire to serve as human torches. And they were boiled in oil and burned at the stake. Historians have estimated that about 5 million Christians were martyred for Christ.

Smyrna needed to see Jesus as the one who had died and come to life again because they would have to be faithful in suffering persecution – even to the point of death. He assured them that they would live forever – get a "crown of life."

Revelation 2: 8-11

[8]"And to the angel of the church in Smyrna write,

"These things says the First and the Last, who was dead, and came to life: [9]"I know your works, tribulation, and poverty (but you are rich); and I know the blasphemy of those who say they are Jews and are not, but are a synagogue of Satan. [10]Do not fear any of those things which you are about to suffer. Indeed, the devil is about to throw some of you into prison, that you may be tested, and you will have tribulation ten days. Be faithful until death, and I will give you the crown of life.

[11]"He who has an ear, let him hear what the Spirit says to the churches. He who overcomes shall not be hurt by the second death.'"

THE CHURCH AT PERGAMUM

Unlike the cities of Ephesus and Smyrna, the city of Pergamum was not known as a commercial city. It had been given a rare gift by the Roman government, the ability to enact capital punishment. Capital punishment was symbolized by the sword in Roman times and the numerous references to swords link the city to capital punishment. Pergamum was also the capital city of Asia until the close of the first century. It was a city given to the worship of many Greek idols. Jesus twice refers to the city as a place where Satan lived and had his throne.

Satan has a kingdom. Babylon has from the earliest times been considered the capital of this kingdom. Idolatry gained its start in Babylon through Nimrod and his wife, inspired by Satan. As long as Babylon was a dominant power, it made an excellent headquarters for Satan's attack on the human race. However when Babylon's glory began to decline and it was left desolate, Satan looked for another location. He selected Pergamum because of its strong idolatrous religions. Christians intermarried with pagans against God's will. Many followed the teaching of the Nicolaitans which was a strong clergy telling people what to do, without people having their own relationship with Christ. No doubt these were the conditions under which the little church of Pergamum was preaching the Gospel of Jesus Christ.

Satan learned from his attack on the church of Smyrna that persecution only causes the church to flourish and continue in a perpetual state of revival. So he changed his strategy to introducing pagan practices. When Constantine became emperor of Rome, he accepted the Christian faith and declared himself to be its defender and protector. During the centuries, however, many anti-Christian practices of pagan origin were adopted, <u>which robbed the church of its fire and its evangelistic fervor</u>. The influence of paganism on the church increased over the years, step-by-step. Gradually these changes became more prominent than the original teachings of Christ.

A.D 300	Prayers for the dead
A.D 300	Making the sign of the cross
A.D 375	Worship saints and angels
A.D 394	Mass first instituted
A.D 431	Worship of Mary begun
A.D 500	Priests began dressing differently than laypeople

A.D 526	Extreme unction
A.D 593	Doctrine of purgatory introduced
A.D 600	Worship services conducted in Latin
A.D 600	Prayers directed to Mary

Jesus gave Pergamum the picture of Himself as *"...Him who has the sharp, double-edged sword"* (i.e. the Word of God) because they were tolerating people teaching heretical doctrine which included sexual immorality. This had to be corrected. If they repented, then the Word would: <u>sanctify them</u> (i.e. separate them from the world and to Himself) - John 17:17, <u>clean them</u> - John 15:3, <u>give them joy</u> - John 15:10-11, and <u>give them peace</u> - John 16:33. But if they didn't repent, they would feel the pain of the other edge of the sword (Revelation 2:16).

The "hidden manna" God promised them for overcoming means that He would sustain them through His Word. They would never be spiritually hungry. But, like the Israelites, <u>the church needed to go out and get it – they needed to seek the truth by searching the Word</u>. The "white stone" Christ promised symbolized being acquitted of a crime. That's what people being tried received if the verdict was "not guilty." It could also stand for God's wholesomeness, holiness, and righteousness. So, because of their faith in Christ, their name would be written in the Book of Life.

Revelation 2: 12-17

[12]"And to the angel of the church in Pergamos write,

"These things says He who has the sharp two-edged sword: [13]"I know your works, and where you dwell, where Satan's throne is. And you hold fast to My name, and did not deny My faith even in the days in which Antipas was My faithful martyr, who was killed among you, where Satan dwells. [14]But I have a few things against you, because you have there those who hold the doctrine of Balaam, who taught Balak to put a stumbling block before the children of Israel, to eat things sacrificed to idols, and to commit sexual immorality. [15]Thus you also have those who hold the doctrine of the Nicolaitans, which thing I hate. ¹⁶Repent, or else I will come to you quickly and will fight against them with the sword of My mouth.

¹⁷"He who has an ear, let him hear what the Spirit says to the churches. To him who overcomes I will give some of the hidden manna to eat. And I will give him a white stone, and on the stone a new name written which no one knows except him who receives it.'"

THE CHURCH AT THYATIRA

The city of Thyatira is the least significant of the seven cities of the seven churches of Revelation. It was away from the main commercial routes. It was small and also didn't hold much religious significance. But it had a big problem. This period in history represents the Church of the Dark Ages. The light that Jesus entrusted to His Church all but flickered out during this time and was not rekindled until the days of the Reformation.
In the verses that follow, Jesus says this church would be inundated with false doctrines and persecuted for her faithfulness to God and His Word. The spirit of compromise that started with Pergamum would reach its zenith in the time of Thyatira. As the name implies ("sweet savor of labor"), works as a means to obtain grace would become a prominent feature of the time.

The following changes and doctrines that have their source in paganism were added to the Church during this period:

A.D 607	Boniface lll made first Pope
A.D 709	Kissing the Pope's foot
A.D 786	Worshiping of images and relics
A.D 850	Use of "holy water" begun
A.D 995	Canonization of dead saints
A.D 998	Fasting on Fridays and during Lent
A.D 1079	Celibacy of the priesthood
A.D 1090	Prayer beads

A.D 1184	The Inquisition
A.D 1190	Sale of indulgences
A.D 1215	Transubstantiation
A.D 1220	Adoration of the wafer
A.D 1229	Bible forbidden to laypeople
A.D 1414	Cup forbidden to people at communion
A.D 1439	Doctrine of purgatory decreed
A.D 1508	The Ave Maria approved

It should also be noted that many remained faithful to the Lord and were martyred because they refused to give up their adherence to the Word of God. It is interesting to note also that Jesus doesn't tell them to leave the church. While the tendency today is to flee to a church that better suits us the moment something goes wrong, the true Christians in this church are instructed to stay where they are. The sinful men and women around them would be removed through judgment.

Thyatira needed to see Jesus as the One with eyes blazing with fire and with feet that were polished by constant friction (i.e. burnished). His fiery eyes displayed His anger over the idolatry and sexual immorality He had to look upon in this church. Rather than correct the false prophetess, this church buried their heads in the sand and pretended they didn't see. Unless they repented, Christ would cause them to suffer intensely. The fire and friction speak volumes about how those who seek righteousness will be persecuted within their own church – much friction against those who point out what needs correction. But they also present the Lord's determination and power to polish them and make them shine brightly again.

Revelation 2: 18-29

[18]"And to the angel of the church in Thyatira write,

"These things says the Son of God, who has eyes like a flame of fire, and His feet like fine brass: [19]"I know your works, love, service, faith, and your patience; and as for your works, the last are more than the first. ²⁰Nevertheless I have a few things against you, because you allow that woman Jezebel, who calls herself a prophetess, to teach and seduce My servants to commit sexual immorality and eat things sacrificed to idols. ²¹And I gave her time to repent of her sexual immorality, and she did not repent. ²²Indeed I will cast her into a sickbed, and those who commit adultery with her into great tribulation, unless they repent of their deeds. ²³I will kill her children with death, and all the churches shall know that I am He who searches the minds and hearts. And I will give to each one of you according to your works.

²⁴"Now to you I say, and to the rest in Thyatira, as many as do not have this doctrine, who have not known the depths of Satan, as they say, I will put on you no other burden. ²⁵But hold fast what you have till I come. ²⁶And he who overcomes, and keeps My works until the end, to him I will give power over the nations--
²⁷"He shall rule them with a rod of iron; They shall be dashed to pieces like the potter's vessels'-- as I also have received from My Father; ²⁸and I will give him the morning star.

²⁹"He who has an ear, let him hear what the Spirit says to the churches.'"

THE CHURCH AT SARDIS

Sardis, the capital city of Lydia, was prominent in Asia Minor and esteemed for its carpet industry. It was a wealthy city that was finally destroyed by an earthquake. The local church there seems to have had an acceptable reputation in certain areas - but was really dead. This is tragic when compared to Jesus saying, *"I have come that they may have life, and have it to the full"* (John 10:10). There were however, a few faithful believers *"in Sardis who have not defiled their garments"* (Revelation 3:4). It's like someone dying of thirst in the desert who sees a well off in the distance, only to find upon arrival that it is dry. Many thirsty souls stumble through the desert of this world and then finally see what they think is hope in the form of a church, only to find upon entering that it is completely dead.

This picture we're given of Sardis represents the Reformation age - and the beginning of the Protestant church. The dark ages of the Roman Catholic Church and her policies was ending. This new time was known as the Renaissance Period. The beginning is said to be 1517 on October 31st, when Martin Luther nailed the 95th thesis to the Wittenberg Castle door. The tragedy of the reformation churches that earned for them the condemnation by the Lord of being "dead" was twofold. First, they became State churches. Luther, for example, sought the approval of the political leaders, and eventually the Lutheran Church became the State Church of Germany. The danger of this is that the church then includes the entire population, thus eliminating the need for personal acceptance of Jesus Christ. Another danger is the tendency to please the government rather than God.

Secondly, the Reformation Church didn't adequately change many customs and teachings of the Church of Rome (e.g. infant baptism, sprinkling, ritualism - including some of the sacraments). Ritualism and formality, characteristic of pagan forms of worship, appeal to our human nature but don't represent genuine worship in Spirit and in Truth. If people leave a church service with a "feeling of worship" but have not been brought face-to-face with Jesus Christ in a personal way, they have been worshipping in a dead church. In Sardis, they had a form of godliness, not the power. They worshipped God, but the spirit was missing. Matthew 15:8-9 says, *"These people honor me with their lips, but their hearts are far from me. They worship me in vain; their teachings are but rules taught by men."* They professed to be Christians but lacked Christ.

Sardis needed to remember Jesus as the One who holds in His hand their leader and the Holy Spirit (i.e. sevenfold Spirit of God). We'll discuss the sevenfold Spirit when John visits God's throne room in a later chapter. Suffice it to say that this represents either the sevenfold gifts of the Spirit in Romans 12: 6-8 or the ministry of the Spirit given in Isaiah 11:2. By portraying Himself this way, Jesus is saying that with the Holy Spirit Sardis can move from being a dead (sleeping) church to one that actively joins the Lord in making disciples. He's holding their leader responsible for proactively teaching the church to remember what they have received and heard, and to repent and obey. If they don't wake up, they will be left behind when Jesus returns to rapture His church (Revelation 3:3).

Revelation 3: 1-6

[1] "And to the angel of the church in Sardis write,

"These things says He who has the seven Spirits of God and the seven stars: "I know your works, that you have a name that you are alive, but you are dead. [2] Be watchful, and strengthen the things which remain, that are ready to die, for I have not found your works perfect before God. [3] Remember therefore how you have received and heard; hold fast and repent. Therefore if you will not watch, I will come upon you as a thief, and you will not know what hour I will come upon you. [4] You have a few names even in Sardis who have not defiled their garments; and they shall walk with Me in white, for they are worthy. [5] He who overcomes shall be clothed in white garments, and I will not blot out his name from the Book of Life; but I will confess his name before My Father and before His angels.

[6] "He who has an ear, let him hear what the Spirit says to the churches.'"

THE CHURCH AT PHILADELPHIA

The name Philadelphia means brotherly love. The city was named after a king who was known for loving his brother. Jesus says nothing bad about this church. <u>They are the church that every church should strive to be like and every member should want to be.</u> Jesus has opened the door to them and no one can shut it. The church of Philadelphia has kept Christ's Word and not denied his name. This church has little strength, but this is a commendation and not a condemnation because they made themselves "perfectly weak" for the Lord to work through them. Genesis 17:1. In today's world, we look at numbers as the source of power but it's this small church that God is commending.

Because of her faithfulness Jesus would make the enemies of Philadelphia fall down at her feet and acknowledge that Jesus loved the church. This church has a powerful testimony in their area for Jesus Christ. We should all strive to live such exemplary lives that no matter how much someone dislikes us, in his heart, he still knows and understands that God loves us. Even though he may not admit it, he will acknowledge that our actions are motivated by our love of Christ. That's the light and life of the Philadelphian church.

The church age represented here is <u>Revival of the Church.</u> The Reformation Church, as we saw became dead and cold as a State church. Philadelphia however was marked by vitality of life. During this church age God worked in a thrilling manner that produced revivals as well as the missionary movement.

The church in Philadelphia needed to see Jesus as holy and true – the One with the golden band (or girdle) of Revelation 1:13 like the belt of truth in Ephesians 6:14. They needed to see Him as the One who never sinned and who keeps His promises - the One who owns the key to every door, and can open or shut them at will. Isaiah 22:22 says, *"I will place on his shoulder the key to the house of David; what he opens no one can shut, and what he shuts no one can open."* Jesus told this church, *"I know your deeds. See, I have placed before you an open door that no one can shut"* (Revelation 3:8). This evidently refers to the doors of opportunity open to them for the proclamation of the gospel, one of the chief characteristics of faithful service throughout this Church age.

This church stood for holiness, and patiently endured hardship (i.e. ambushes) coming from those who claimed to be friends but were deceivers working for the enemy. Because they stood the testing of their faith, He would keep them from the great tribulation coming to test the inhabitants of earth (Revelation 3:10). He promises to make them a pillar forever in God's temple (Revelation 3:11) – for all to admire Christ's redeeming work. He also promises them in verse 11 that He is coming soon. He also promises them a crown. And in verse 12, He further promises to write the name of His God, His city, and His new name on them.

Revelation 3: 7-13

⁷"And to the angel of the church in Philadelphia write,

"These things says He who is holy, He who is true, "He who has the key of David, He who opens and no one shuts, and shuts and no one opens": ⁸"I know your works. See, I have set before you an open door, and no one can shut it; for you have a little strength, have kept My word, and have not denied My name. ⁹Indeed I will make those of the synagogue of Satan, who say they are Jews and are not, but lie--indeed I will make them come and worship before your feet, and to know that I have loved you. ¹⁰Because you have kept My command to persevere, I also will keep you from the hour of trial which shall come upon the whole world, to test those who dwell on the earth. ¹¹Behold, I am coming quickly! Hold fast what you have, that no one may take your crown. ¹²He who overcomes, I will make him a pillar in the temple of My God, and he shall go out no more. I will write on him the name of My God and the name of the city of My God, the New Jerusalem, which comes down out of heaven from My God. And I will write on him My new name.

¹³"He who has an ear, let him hear what the Spirit says to the churches."'

THE CHURCH AT LAODICEA

The city of Laodicea was the wealthiest in the province of Asia Minor and was well known for its banking industry, medical school, and textile industry. It was also known for its lack of good drinking water. This is the church that made Jesus sick. The word

"Laodicea" means "the people rule." Nicolaitanism is to rule <u>over</u> the people. Laodiceanism is for the people to rule over themselves. This name represents the spirit of this age in a special way. It's about "people's rights" (i.e. "Nobody has the right to tell me what to do and what I can not do").

If the report on the church of Philadelphia was all good, then the report on the church of Laodicea was all bad. <u>Jesus has nothing good to say about this church</u> as it is the opposite of the Philadelphian church is many ways. At least the church of Sardis had a false reputation for being alive. The church of Laodicea did not fool anyone.

Jesus calls the church lukewarm and warns that he is about to spit them out of his mouth. This is a reference to the quality of drinking water in the area to which the church would have been able to identify. The church of Laodicea is a large church. They are wealthy. They have no trouble meeting their budget every month. They say to themselves, "I am rich, and have acquired wealth and do not need a thing." What they need is Jesus.

This age of the church represents the "<u>Worldly Church</u>" - corrupt Christianity (1900-? AD). The turn of the century saw great changes taking place both in the world and in the church. Not only were there new bibles and new religions, but the Church began to compromise with paganism again. Biblical standards fall as worldliness corrupts the minds of believers. Faith is undermined, eventually resulting in the "God is dead" mentality of the 1960's. The Word of God is replaced with a powerless gospel in many churches, who now rely upon gimmicks rather than the Living Word. The Laodicean age is one of spiritual lukewarmness and Christless Christianity.

Look at the Laodicean church through the Lord's eyes. Remember Christ sees all and will reveal all. In Revelation 3:17, Christ calls her **"wretched, miserable"** - Inwardly her people were an unhappy, wretched lot, for riches never satisfy the hungry human heart; **"poor"** - Even though rich in material things, the Laodicean church members were poor because they did not know Christ. *"What good is it for a man to gain the whole world, yet forfeit his soul?"* Mark 8:36; **"blind"** – All their education and sophistication couldn't teach them God's ways; **"naked"** - This 21st century Laodicean church is clothed with religion. She wraps herself in religious robes, burns her candles, waves her symbols, offers her chants, and reads her creeds; but our Lord sees her as "naked". She's not wrapped in faith to produce garments of righteousness and holiness.

Laodicea needed to see Jesus as the Amen. It's a Hebrew word that means "true" and carries with it the meaning of finality (i.e.. the One who declares "it is done"). In this sense, Christ is the final truth. That is, all God's revelations to humankind about Himself are found in the person of Jesus Christ. If you want to know about God, all you have to do is study the life of Jesus Christ.

They also needed to see Jesus as the faithful and true witness, the ruler of God's creation. Because this church wouldn't take a stand for Jesus – His being the Only Way to the Father and being our Righteousness - and didn't seek His kingdom first, Jesus was about to spit the bad taste of them out of His mouth. Wealth (mammon) was this church's god, and it had made them very comfortable and complacent. Jesus reminded them that He owned their wealth and everything else in creation – He can give and He can take away. Being a faithful, true witness of God's love through Christ despite shame and persecution was to have real riches – *"But my God shall supply all your need according to His riches in glory by Christ Jesus."* Philippians 4:19. He told them that they still had time to acknowledge Him before men and He would acknowledge them at God's throne (3:19-21). It was their choice!

Revelation 3: 14-22

[14]"And to the angel of the church of the Laodiceans write,

"These things says the Amen, the Faithful and True Witness, the Beginning of the creation of God: [15]"I know your works, that you are neither cold nor hot. I could wish you were cold or hot. ^{16}So then, because you are lukewarm, and neither cold nor hot, I will vomit you out of My mouth. ^{17}Because you say, "I am rich, have become wealthy, and have need of nothing'--and do not know that you are wretched, miserable, poor, blind, and naked-- ^{18}I counsel you to buy from Me gold refined in the fire, that you may be rich; and white garments, that you may be clothed, that the shame of your nakedness may not be revealed; and anoint your eyes with eye salve, that you may see. ^{19}As many as I love, I rebuke and chasten. Therefore be zealous and repent. ^{20}Behold, I stand at the door and knock. If anyone hears My voice and opens the door, I will come in to him and dine with him, and he with Me. ^{21}To him who overcomes I will grant to sit with Me on My throne, as I also overcame and sat down with My Father on His throne.

^{22}"He who has an ear, let him hear what the Spirit says to the churches."''

Looking to Jesus, my spirit is blest,
The world is in turmoil, in Him I have rest;
The sea of my life around me may roar,
When I look to Jesus, I hear it no more.
- *Anonymous*

CHAPTER 4
SATAN CAST TO EARTH & UNRESTRAINED LAWLESSNESS

John sees Israel depicted as a woman with a crown of twelve stars. These stars probably represent the 12 patriarchs and heads of the twelve tribes of Israel. She is clothed with the sun because the light of God (i.e. His Word) was given to her as well as The Light of the World (i.e. Jesus Christ). He's the man child born to the woman and taken up to be at the right hand of God on His throne. Additionally, this vision represents the reality that Christ as Messiah is being "born" in the hearts of a remnant of Jews from the twelve tribes at this time. In Revelation 7: 4-8, we will see that God uses some 144,000 Jews to evangelize and prepare others of Israel for receiving Christ as Messiah.

The dragon is Satan, who rebelled against God's plan for his life. Spiritual warfare ensued from creation until now. See Appendix B. Satan has been trying to prevent man from being in a right relationship with God – for many years trying to prevent the Seed of the woman, promised by God in the Garden of Eden, from coming. Once He did come, born of a virgin, being sacrificed for the sins of the world, and being raised from the dead to give new life to all who would accept Him, Satan has been deceiving people from believing in Him.

He is depicted here as a dragon with seven heads, each with a crown, and one head with ten horns. He appears to be a political figure who "spews water" (i.e. a clever tongue) to sweep away the woman. But others on earth (probably politicians as well) help the woman by opening its mouth to swallow up the dragon's words. The seven heads represent seven kingdoms of the earth that contained the nation of Israel: Egypt, Assyria, Babylon, Media-Persia, Greco-Macedonia, Rome, and one that will shortly appear headed by the Antichrist. We will discuss this further when we deal with the rise of the Antichrist.

As we see in the book of Job, Satan had been permitted by God to have entrance into heaven. But now, he and his demons are confined to the earth because his end is very near. As we shall see, Satan inspires the Antichrist to make a 7-year peace treaty with Israel but breaks it after 3 ½ years. For the next 3 ½ years, there is a remnant of Jews that comes to believe in Christ as Messiah (i.e. bring forth a man child), who are protected from Satan and the Antichrist, and also from God's wrath, while God "nourishes" that belief and prepares them to meet Christ when He returns to rule earth with a "rod of iron."

"And to the woman were given two wings of a great eagle, that she might fly into the wilderness…" (12:6). This special protection by the Lord for Israel is not new. *"You yourselves have seen what I did to Egypt, and how I carried you on eagles' wings and brought you to myself."* Exodus 19:4. Many believe that the "wilderness" where the woman (i.e. Israel) goes to be protected is an ancient city called Sela (the rock city). Its modern name is Petra in Jordan. See Isaiah 16:1-5. Verses 4-5 say to Sela, *"<u>Let mine outcasts dwell with thee, Moab; be thou a covert to them from the face of the spoiler: for the extortioner is at an end, the spoiler ceaseth, the oppressors are consumed out of the land</u>. And in mercy shall the throne be established: and he shall sit upon it in truth in the tabernacle of David, judging, and seeking judgment, and hasting righteousness."*

Revelation 12:1 - 17

[1] Now a great sign appeared in heaven: a woman clothed with the sun, with the moon under her feet, and on her head a garland of twelve stars. [2] Then being with child, she cried out in labor and in pain to give birth.

[3] And another sign appeared in heaven: behold, a great, fiery red dragon having seven heads and ten horns, and seven diadems on his heads. [4] His tail drew a third of the stars of heaven and threw them to the earth. And the dragon stood before the woman who

was ready to give birth, to devour her Child as soon as it was born. ⁵She bore a male Child who was to rule all nations with a rod of iron. And her Child was caught up to God and His throne. ⁶Then the woman fled into the wilderness, where she has a place prepared by God, that they should feed her there one thousand two hundred and sixty days.

⁷And war broke out in heaven: Michael and his angels fought with the dragon; and the dragon and his angels fought, ⁸but they did not prevail, nor was a place found for them in heaven any longer. ⁹So the great dragon was cast out, that serpent of old, called the Devil and Satan, who deceives the whole world; he was cast to the earth, and his angels were cast out with him.

¹⁰Then I heard a loud voice saying in heaven, "Now salvation, and strength, and the kingdom of our God, and the power of His Christ have come, for the accuser of our brethren, who accused them before our God day and night, has been cast down. ¹¹And they overcame him by the blood of the Lamb and by the word of their testimony, and they did not love their lives to the death. ¹²Therefore rejoice, O heavens, and you who dwell in them! Woe to the inhabitants of the earth and the sea! For the devil has come down to you, having great wrath, because he knows that he has a short time."

¹³Now when the dragon saw that he had been cast to the earth, he persecuted the woman who gave birth to the male Child. ¹⁴But the woman was given two wings of a great eagle, that she might fly into the wilderness to her place, where she is nourished for a time and times and half a time, from the presence of the serpent. ¹⁵So the serpent spewed water out of his mouth like a flood after the woman, that he might cause her to be carried away by the flood. ¹⁶But the earth helped the woman, and the earth opened its mouth and swallowed up the flood which the dragon had spewed out of his mouth. ¹⁷And the dragon was enraged with the woman, and he went to make war with the rest of her offspring, who keep the commandments of God and have the testimony of Jesus Christ.

The God who made the firmament,
Who made the deepest sea,
The God who put the stars in place
Is the God who cares for me.
  - Berg

CHAPTER 5
THE RAPTURE OF THE CHURCH

During this battle with Satan, who is called the Prince of the Air, while Archangel Michael and his angel army have them occupied, he gives a "shout" – that all *"principalities, powers, rulers of darkness...spiritual wickedness in high places"* have been contained. See Ephesians 6:12. So there should be no more delay for the Church to be extracted from earth. It may seem strange to us that Satan and his armies need to be restrained before we can *"meet the Lord in the air."* 1 Thessalonians 4:17. But remember that God's angel was *"resisted twenty-one days"* by the *"prince of the Persian kingdom"* trying to get a message to Daniel until *"Michael, one of the chief princes"*, came to help him. Daniel 10:13.

Christ has warned the Church of the consequences of not being prepared, and He has encouraged them to stand firm for Him in the face of persecution and apostasy from within. As we read Revelation 4:1, the Apostle John now represents the Body of

Christ being taken up to heaven in what we call the Rapture. *"But I would not have you to be ignorant, brethren concerning them which are asleep, that ye sorrow not, even as others which have no hope. For if we believe that Jesus died and rose again, even so them also which sleep in Jesus will God bring with Him. For this we say unto you by the word of the Lord, that we which are alive and remain unto the coming of the Lord shall not prevent them which are asleep. <u>For the Lord himself shall descend from heaven with a shout, with the voice</u>*

of the archangel, and with the trump of God: and the dead in Christ shall rise first: Then we which are alive and remain shall be caught up together with them in the clouds, to meet the Lord in the air: and so shall we ever be with the Lord." 1 Thessalonians 4: 17-19.

In the twinkling of an eye, those who are dead in Christ receive immortal bodies and rise first to meet the Lord. Then those who are alive at this time receive incorruptible bodies and also rise to meet the Lord in the air and forever be with Him. 1 Corinthians 15:52-53 says, *"...in a flash, in the twinkling of an eye, at the last trumpet. For the trumpet will sound, the dead will be raised imperishable, and we shall be changed. For the perishable must clothe itself with the imperishable, and the mortal with immortality."*

In Matthew 24:3, Jesus' disciples asked Him about the signs and time of His return. They also asked for the signs of the end of the age. His answers show that His coming would be in two phases. See Appendix A. Verses 3-14 give the signs of the first phase we call the "rapture": False "christs" v. 5; Wars and rumors of wars v.7; Pestilences and earthquakes v.7; Persecution v.9; Defections from the faith vs. 10-13; Worldwide preaching of the gospel v. 14. Near-at-hand and far-off elements are blended together – so to those believers who lived and died under terrible persecution, "the end" in v. 13 is the end of life. But to those who live during the coming Tribulation, it will be the end of the age. To first century "preaching the gospel" was to the Roman world. Today it's the whole earth.

Christ's answer to when this phase would occur is given in Matthew 24:36-51: That day would catch people by surprise v.36. It would be like the days of Noah - everyone would go about business as usual because they didn't believe the flood would really come vs. 37-39. He also said that two people will be together in various places and *"one will be taken, and the other left"* vs. 40-41. And finally He warned them, *"Therefore you also be ready, for the Son of Man is coming at an hour when you do not expect Him"* v.44.

The second phase of Christ's coming is evident by His answer concerning the signs of the end of the age. They are given in Matthew 24: 15-35. Jesus said that there would be enough fear to drive the Jews to the hills vs. 16-18. There would be unparalleled trouble and woe vs. 19-20. Great tribulation would threaten all life if the days were not shortened vs. 21-22. False christs and prophets would be there vs. 23-26. The end of the age would see startling celestial signs and the visible descent of the Son of Man *"with power and great glory"* vs.29-31. He said that like the appearing of buds on trees signal summer, these signs signal that the end of the age is *"near, at the very doors"* v33. The Jews to whom Jesus was speaking knew that Daniel 9:24-27 foretold of a hostile Gentile ruler (the Antichrist in Revelation) who would someday desecrate the temple and bring terrible persecution. Jesus told them the generation that sees the beginning of the desecration of the temple (v. 15) will not pass away <u>before the Lord returns</u>. v.34.

The word "rapture" is not mentioned in scripture. It comes from the Latin "rapere" which means *"snatch away"* or *"be caught up"*. By "rapture" we mean "the taking home of the Church." It's the <u>first phase</u> of Christ's coming back. It is the fulfillment of Jesus' promise to His disciples. *"Let not your heart be troubled: ye believe in God, believe also in me. In my Father's house are many mansions (i.e. great rooms): if it were not so, I would have told you. I go to prepare a place for you. And if I go and prepare a place for you, I will come again, and receive you unto unto myself; that where I am, there ye may be also."* John 14: 1-3. You might say that just like the disciples prepared an upper room for Christ, likewise Christ is preparing an upper room for His disciples!

If there were no rapture in our future, we would have to spend eternity without a body! We must receive a new immortal body to enjoy all that Christ has prepared for us in heaven and on earth. Christians who have died are now in heaven (the paradise Christ promised the thief on the cross). But they do not yet have their resurrected bodies. At the Rapture, their spirits and souls descend to meet their transformed bodies.

The <u>first rapture</u> is given in Genesis 5:24, *"Enoch walked with God; and he was not, for God took (i.e. raptured) him."* Enoch spoke about the <u>second phase</u> of Christ's coming (i.e. at the Battle of Armageddon). Jude 14-15 says, *"Enoch…prophesied…saying, 'Behold the Lord comes <u>with ten thousands of His saints</u>, to execute judgment on all…ungodly…'"* He also prophesied the judgment that was to come through the flood, not in his lifetime, but after his son Methuselah died. "Methuselah" means *after he goes, then it happens*. When Enoch was 365 years old, God took him before His judgment fell on the evil people of that day. This is an example of how God first delivers a prophetic warning, then removes the righteous and finally delivers the judgment! This is what He will do at the Rapture – remove the righteous.

There was a <u>second rapture</u> recorded in scripture. It was when God took Elijah to heaven by a chariot of fire and a whirlwind. *"And it came to pass, as they (i.e. Elijah and Elisha) still went on, and talked, that, behold there appeared a chariot of fire, and horses of fire, and parted them both asunder; and Elijah went up by a whirlwind into heaven."* 2 Kings 2:11.

It is now by God's grace through John that we (the Church) get to see the future from a perspective that requires us to have perfect vision – vision that requires time to stand still so we can take a snapshot of the future quickly as only the Lord can. John is told in Revelation 10 to eat a little book, which is this Book of Revelation, so he can give the Church this heavenly vision.

Revelation 4:1

[1] After these things I looked, and behold, a door standing open in heaven. And the first voice which I heard was like a trumpet

speaking with me, saying, "Come up here, and I will show you things which must take place after this."

MORE INFORMATION FROM SCRIPTURE

Luke 17:26-30 – *"Just as it was in the days of Noah, so also will it be in the days of the Son of Man. People were eating, drinking, marrying and being given in marriage up to the day Noah entered the ark. Then the flood came and destroyed them all. It was the same in the days of Lot. People were eating, drinking, buying, selling, planting and building. But the day Lot left Sodom, fire and sulfur rained down from heaven and destroyed them all. It will be just like this on the day the Son of Man is revealed."*

2 Thessalonians 2: 3-10 – *"Let no man deceive you by any means: for that day shall not come, except there be a falling away first, and that man of sin be revealed, the son of perdition; Who opposeth and exalteth himself above all that is called God, or that is worshipped; so that he as God sitteth in the temple of God, shewing himself that he is God. Remember ye not, that, when I was yet with you, I told you these things? And now ye know what withholdeth that he might be revealed in his time. For the mystery of iniquity doth already work: only he who now letteth will let, until he be taken out of the way. And then shall that Wicked be revealed, whom the Lord shall consume with the spirit of his mouth, and shall destroy with the brightness of his coming: Even him, whose coming is after the working of Satan with all power and signs and lying wonders, And with all deceivableness of unrighteousness in them that perish; because they revealed not the love of the truth, that they might be saved."*

Who measures how we've done in life
And judges our success?
Our God, who gives rewards to those
Who live in righteousness.
- Branon

CHAPTER 6
THE JUDGMENT SEAT OF CHRIST

We Christians *"must all appear before the judgment seat of Christ."* 2 Corinthians 5: 10. Have you ever wondered how we who have been serving Christ would be judged? Here's a vision (a dream) I received concerning what this Judgment Seat of Christ might be all about…

One summer day, I was invited to address 60 pastors and leaders of a major denomination. It was exciting for me to think about what might result from giving "seed" to these "sowers" of the Gospel. That afternoon, the Virginia sun was burning brightly and I decided to rest a while. As I contemplated what the Lord had given me to say, I fell into a deep sleep. Immediately, I was launched into a heavenly realm where I stood with ten thousand times ten thousand and thousands of thousands. They were from *every kindred, tongue, people, and nation.* In the midst of these vast numbers of people stood a Judgment Seat and there in all His glory was Christ, Himself. At first, He was so bright that I couldn't tell it was Him; but it soon became apparent that this Glorious Person was my Lord. All the people praised Him and the sound of their cheers was deafening.

I joined in the singing and praising. Then something very strange happened. Jesus looked at me. It seemed that the Lord's eye caught the eye of everyone at the same time. It was probably like what happened to Peter – after he had denied the Lord three times – when Jesus looked at me. The noise of the crowd seemed to hush and I could only see Christ's eye. The Lord's look must have only lasted a moment, but it seemed to me like a lifetime. I'd experienced being heart-to-heart with the Lord, but now we were eye-to-eye.

I was lifted to spiritual heights unknown to me till now. I saw a stability -surpassing the tallest of earth's mountains; a strength –

surpassing the combined force of the wind and ocean during a violent storm; a purity - surpassing the smallest of infants; a peace - surpassing the most tranquil waters; a deep, genuine care and concern – surpassing a mother's love for her nursing child; a joy - surpassing a father who receives back his rebellious son; and, a hope - surpassing the runner about to pass the finish line first.

With that look, it seemed the Lord searched to see His own image in me. Though Jesus was looking at me for a reflection of Himself, I began to see myself reflected back to me. I began to see certain events from my life - they were opportunities I had missed to share the Gospel or to emulate Christ – they were times when I'd worked for Christ in my own strength and not in His strength. Tears flowed over my face as I viewed these things – because I saw them being burned up like wood, hay, and stubble.

Then my eyes, as if controlled by a source outside myself, viewed more and more of the Lord's face – not just His eye. When I caught a glimpse of His mouth, the Lord began to smile with such warmth that my tears were dried up instantly and I began to feel a certain glow about me. Then the Lord called me by a new name I'd never heard before and said, *"Enter the joy of your Lord* and let me show you the meaning of your life." When I heard the Lord call me by that new name I was puzzled because many years before, I heard the Lord call me "Jim". Knowing this, Jesus explained, "I called you "Jim" when you were searching to know Me. You still were living for yourself. You still had the "I" in the center of your life. But as you allowed yourself to be transformed, My name for you became "Jjom", because you put Me (Jesus) and Others in the center instead of yourself!"

And then the Lord put me into an inverted pyramid with others whom I recognized and knew during my lifetime. See Appendix A. They were all arranged into an upside down pyramid with me at the very bottom. The Lord then pointed to each one of these people and began to tell me what happened to them. The Lord began, "Do you remember this lady who was on the bus, who was almost ready to deny My existence? You ran after her, witnessed

to her, and she received Me there in the parking lot. Do you
remember? She became a Sunday school teacher and led many
children to accept me also." And as He spoke those children – that
I'd never met - were added to the pyramid. "Remember this young
man in your singles group who became a pastor? He got a church
in the inner city and he was put in charge of inner city ministry on
the United States East coast. He made disciples who also went on
to bring My gospel to many inner city people." When He said that,
more people that I'd never met were added and the pyramid got
even bigger. Then pointing to a group of people who were with
me in the pyramid, the Lord said, "Do you remember these sixty
people who accepted Me during the lay witness mission that you
led? They each brought one more to me." And more people were
added to the pyramid.

The Lord continued to tell me about the young soldier, who I had
helped find his way back to Christ, the lesbian, who had accepted
Him and became a Sunday school teacher, all the members of my
Sunday school classes, workshops, and seminars. There were
many that I had touched but was unaware of – some were children
of parents I'd helped stay together – others were people I'd prayed
for unceasingly, not knowing any of the results.

As I looked at everyone in the pyramid above me, I remembered
what the Apostle Paul had told the Thessalonians, *"For what is our
hope, our joy, or the crown in which we will glory in the presence
of our Lord Jesus Christ when he comes? Is it not you? Indeed,
you are our glory and joy."* 1 Thessalonians 2:19-20. I realized
that the Lord had created a crown of rejoicing people all around
me!

When the Lord finished speaking with me, I noticed that I was not
at the very bottom of this crown. Esther, the woman who led me to
Christ, was under me. And I was only a small part of her crown.
Under her was another, and another further down, and that
continued further and further downward. At the very bottom of the
pyramid, with an uncountable number in the crown, was Christ.
He had the greatest and largest crown! He said, "Do you

remember when I told you that if you would be the greatest in My kingdom, you should be the servant of all? I told you, *"Whosoever desires to be first among you, let him be your slave – just as the Son of Man did not come to be served but to serve, and to give his life a ransom for many."* I realized that Jesus was First and Last – that He was the Source as well as the Finish Line of my faith. But there was something even below Christ. I realized, after a while of straining to see, that at the very bottom of the crown was the image of a broken heart – it was the Father's broken heart. But His heart was healed!

Suddenly, I felt another crown upon my head and the Lord said, "Behold your hope, and joy, and crown of rejoicing. Are not these people, to whom you ministered, who are now in My presence, your hope, joy, and crown?" Then without delay I cast my crown at the Lord's feet and these words fell effortlessly from my lips, *"You alone are worthy, O Lord, to receive the glory and honor and power."* Immediately the space around me became brilliant with light. And I remembered what Daniel had said, *"They that turn many to righteousness shall shine as the stars for ever and ever."* See Daniel 12:3.

When I awoke, I fell to my knees and rededicated my life to Christ. I asked forgiveness for not using every opportunity the Lord had given me to share Christ with others. I asked forgiveness for the times I "lived by flesh" rather than living by faith and trust in Christ. I wanted more than ever before to tell people about Him – His stability, strength, purity, love, joy, peace, and hope – to tell Christians about their appointment with Him at the Judgment Seat. I started by telling the pastors I was speaking with that day and they went on to sow that seed in many other hearts. I'm sure I'll meet them all on that great Judgment Seat day in my *crown of rejoicing*!

Do you want to rededicate your life to Him? Do you want to "touch" others for the Lord by His power and not in your own flesh? Do you want to be a source of light to others, and allow the Lord to lead and guide your life? Do you want to be ready for His return? In the stillness of your heart, sincerely tell Him so. Then you can say, like me, *"Even so, come Lord Jesus."*

Revelation 4: 2 - 3

²Immediately I was in the Spirit; and behold, a throne set in heaven, and One sat on the throne. ³And He who sat there was like a jasper and a sardius stone in appearance; and there was a rainbow around the throne, in appearance like an emerald.

MORE INFORMATION FROM SCRIPTURE

2 Corinthians 5: 10 For we must all appear before the judgment seat of Christ; that every one may receive the things done in his body, according to that he hath done, whether it be good or bad.

1Corinthians 3: 11-15 For other foundation can no man lay than that is laid, which is Jesus Christ. Now if any man build upon this foundation gold, silver, precious stones, wood, hay, stubble; Every man's work shall be made manifest: for the day shall declare it, because it shall be revealed by fire; and the fire shall try every man's work of what sort it is. If any man's work abide which he hath build, thereupon, he shall receive a reward. If any man's work shall be burned, he shall suffer loss: but he himself shall be saved; yet so as by fire.

Matthew 25:14-30 For the kingdom of heaven is as a man traveling into far country, who called his own servants, and delivered unto them his goods. And unto one he gave five talents, to another two, and to another one; to every man according to his ability; and straightway took his journey. Then he that had received five talents went and traded with the same, and made them other five talents. And likewise he that had received two, he also gained other two. But he that had received one went and digged in the earth, and hid his Lord's money.

50 – What's In <u>Your</u> Future?

After a long time the lord of those servants cometh and reckoneth with them. And so he that had received five talents came and brought other five talents, saying, Lord, thou deliverest unto me five talents: behold, I have gained beside them five talents more. His lord said unto him, Well done, thou good and faithful servant: thou hast been faithful over a few things, I will make thee ruler over many things: enter thou into the joy of thy lord. He also that had received two talents came and said, Lord, thou deliverest unto me two talents: behold I have gained two other talents beside them. His lord said unto him, Well done, good and faithful servant; thou hast been faithful in few things, I will make thee ruler over many things: enter thou into the joy of thy lord.

Then he which had received the one talent came and said, Lord, I knew thee that thou art a hard man, reaping where thou hast not sown, and gathering where thou hast not strawed: And I was afraid, and went and hid thy talent in the earth: lo, there thou hast that is thine. His lord answered and said unto him, Thou wicked and slothful servant, thou knewest that I reap where I sowed not, and gather where I have not strawed: Thou oughtest therefore to have put my money to the exchangers, and then at my coming I should have received mine own with usury. Take therefore the talent from him, and give it to him which hath ten talents. For unto everyone that hath shall be given, and he shall have abundance: but from him that hath not shall be taken away even that which he hath. And cast ye the unprofitable servant into outer darkness: there shall be weeping and gnashing of teeth.

Here are the 5 "crowns" of Scripture:
Crown of Life for withstanding tribulation – Rev 2:10
Crown of Glory for elders and pastors – 1 Peter 5: 1-4
Crown of Rejoicing for faithful witnessing – 1 Thessalonians 2:19
Crown of Righteousness for those who long for Christ's return – 2Timothy 4:8
Incorruptible Crown for overcoming the daily struggles – 1 Corinthians 9:25

Revelation 4:4

⁴Around the throne were twenty-four thrones, and on the thrones I saw twenty-four elders sitting, clothed in white robes; and they had crowns of gold on their heads.

So amid the conflict, whether great or small,
Do not be discouraged – God is over all;
Count your many blessings – angels will attend,
Help and comfort give you to your journey's end.
- Oatman

CHAPTER 7
THE RISE OF THE ANTICHRIST WORLD RULER AND HIS PROPHET

John sees a beast rise out of the sea with seven heads with ten horns, each one having a crown on it. We refer to this beast as the Antichrist. We can see that he is in the image of Satan (i.e. the dragon of Revelation 12). We learn that the dragon gives this beast his power. As with the dragon, this Antichrist has 7 heads representing the seven kingdoms of Egypt, Assyria, Babylonia, Media-Persia, Greco-Macedonia, Rome, and his present kingdom.

One of the heads of the beast seemed to have had a fatal wound, but the fatal wound had been healed. This "fatal wound" for the Antichrist was when Christ, during the Roman Empire, became a Spotless Offering to God for the sins of the whole world. All who accept Christ as Savior and Lord are delivered from God's sentence for sin - eternal death. They have new life in Christ (1 Corinthians 1:30). This was a death blow to Satan and the "Satan-Man", Antichrist, because the resulting kingdom of believers would seek first the kingdom of God and His righteousness, which prevented lawlessness (and the Antichrist) until it was taken out of the way.

2 Thessalonians 2:7 speaks of the rapture of the Church, *"For the secret power of lawlessness is already at work; but the one (i.e. the Church) who now holds it back will continue to do so till he is taken out of the way."* In the Garden of Eden, God told Satan, *"he (i.e. the seed of the woman) will crush your head, and you will strike his heel."* See Genesis 3:15. But then came the apostasy – falling away – of the Church: *"Let no man deceive you by any means: for that day (i.e. the day of Christ's return) shall not come, except there come a falling away first, and that man of sin be revealed, the son of perdition (i.e. the Antichrist)."* What could have been a fatal wound was given new life.

One of the heads (i.e. the last kingdom) has 10 horns. To understand this more fully, we need to study the visions of Daniel as well as his interpretation of Nebuchadnezzar's dream as follows:

Daniel 2: 31-45 shows the statue of Nebuchadnezzar's dream having 5 kingdoms beginning at Babylon. The next three are Media-Persia, Greco-Macedonia, and Rome. The 5th is a kingdom that lasts for a short time made up of 10 toes of iron and clay. These are probably the 10 kings of Revelation 13, who can't maintain unity because some are Muslim and some non-Muslim. A great stone cut out by God's hand crushes these "toes", causing all the other kingdoms to collapse, and grows into a great mountain and fills the whole earth (i.e. Christ's rule).

Daniel 7: 1-27 speaks of four beasts coming up out of the sea: One was like a lion with wings of an eagle (i.e. Babylon). One was like a bear with three ribs in its mouth (i.e. Media-Persia). One was like a leopard, with four wings and four heads (i.e. Greco-Macedonia). The beast of Revelation 13:2 resembles a leopard; has feet like a bear; and, a mouth like a lion. Therefore, the Antichrist will speak like Babylon (i.e. the present day Iraq); take actions like Media-Persia (i.e. the present day Iran); and, appear like a Greco-Macedonian (i.e. possibly Syria).

The 4th kingdom of Daniel 7 (i.e. Rome) is *"different from all the other kingdoms and devours the whole earth, trampling it down and crushing it."* Daniel 7:23. This probably has reference to its pervasive immorality, materialism, lust for dominance over others, and idolatry. These attributes of man have endured to this day because (it seems) anything it touched was held in its grasp because of its *"large iron teeth."* It also had 10 horns, which represent ten kings who will arise out of the kingdom. After them another king arises (i.e. the Antichrist) who oppresses the saints and tries to change the set times and laws. *"But the court will sit, and his (Antichrist) power will be taken away and completely destroyed forever. Then the sovereignty, power and greatness of the kingdoms under the whole heaven will be handed over to the*

The Rise of the Antichrist World Ruler and His Prophet

saints, the people of the Most High." Daniel 7:26-27. *"...one like a son of man, coming with the clouds of heaven...was given authority, glory, and sovereign power; all peoples, nations, and men of every language worshipped him. His dominion is an everlasting dominion that will not pass away..."* Daniel 7:14.

Revelation 13: 1-5

¹ Then I stood on the sand of the sea. And I saw a beast rising up out of the sea, having seven heads and ten horns, and on his horns ten crowns, and on his heads a blasphemous name. ²Now the beast which I saw was like a leopard, his feet were like the feet of a bear, and his mouth like the mouth of a lion. The dragon gave him his power, his throne, and great authority. ³And I saw one of his heads as if it had been mortally wounded, and his deadly wound was healed. And all the world marveled and followed the beast. ⁴So they worshiped the dragon who gave authority to the beast; and they worshiped the beast, saying, "Who is like the beast? Who is able to make war with him?"

⁵And he was given a mouth speaking great things and blasphemies, and he was given authority to continue for forty-two months.

John begins to reveal the global influence of the Antichrist – that he will have power over all people, and even make war with God's people and overcome them. There are organizations that for many years have been preparing for this world leadership:

- The Council on Foreign Relations (CFR) is committed to the elimination of national boundaries and merging of all nation states into a one world government.
- The purpose of the Trilateral Commission (TC) and the CFR is to infiltrate and dominate the decision-making bodies of government. They use the academic community and the media to influence key people to adopt a new world order (NWO) philosophy.

- A third secret group behind the rush toward world government is the Bilderberg Group founded in 1954. This group's purpose is to create the European portion of the NWO plan to create the European community. They are also closely tied to the CFR and TC. Their members hold some of the highest governmental and industrial positions - making it possible to infiltrate and promote their views.
- The Club of Rome was formed in 1968 as a European "think-tank" to study various complicated issues involved in preparing the nations to accept the coming NWO. The Club of Rome has used its studies and reports to promote the belief that the only way out of our intractable problems is to abandon our national sovereignty to a world government. Their studies present massive world problems and offer world government as the only possible solution.
- Another feature of this planned restructuring of the world involves the coercion by the World Bank and international Monetary Fund to force developing countries to follow the rules of the New World Order. These international institutions use the "carrot" of new loans and the "stick" of approval of dept-restructuring to force third world countries into their assigned positions in the New World Order.

Revelation 13: 6-10

[6] Then he opened his mouth in blasphemy against God, to blaspheme His name, His tabernacle, and those who dwell in heaven. [7] It was granted to him to make war with the saints and to overcome them. And authority was given him over every tribe, tongue, and nation. [8] All who dwell on the earth will worship him, whose names have not been written in the Book of Life of the Lamb slain from the foundation of the world.

[9] If anyone has an ear, let him hear. [10] He who leads into captivity shall go into captivity; he who kills with the sword must be killed with the sword. Here is the patience and the faith of the saints.

John now sees another beast. This one seemed to have a religious purpose because it causes those who dwell in the earth to worship the first beast. He is called the False Prophet (Revelation 19:20). So what Satan has manufactured is a counterfeit trinity: He's put himself in the Father's place; the Antichrist in the Son's place; and, the False Prophet in the Holy Spirit's place.

Revelation 13: 11-17

^{11}Then I saw another beast coming up out of the earth, and he had two horns like a lamb and spoke like a dragon. ^{12}And he exercises all the authority of the first beast in his presence, and causes the earth and those who dwell in it to worship the first beast, whose deadly wound was healed. ^{13}He performs great signs, so that he even makes fire come down from heaven on the earth in the sight of men. ^{14}And he deceives those who dwell on the earth by those signs which he was granted to do in the sight of the beast, telling those who dwell on the earth to make an image to the beast who was wounded by the sword and lived. ^{15}He was granted power to give breath to the image of the beast, that the image of the beast should both speak and cause as many as would not worship the image of the beast to be killed. ^{16}He causes all, both small and great, rich and poor, free and slave, to receive a mark on their right hand or on their foreheads, ^{17}and that no one may buy or sell except one who has the mark or the name of the beast, or the number of his name.

MORE INFORMATION FROM SCRIPTURE

The Antichrist will establish a treaty with Israel for 7 years. But after 3 ½ years, it will be broken. Daniel 9: 27 – *"He (Antichrist) will confirm a covenant with many for one 'seven'. In the middle of the 'seven' he will put an end to sacrifice and offering. And on a wing of the temple he will set up an abomination that causes desolation, until the end that is decreed is poured out on him."*

Daniel 11:36-38 - *And the king (Antichrist) shall do according to his will; and he shall exalt himself, and magnify himself above every god, and shall speak marvelous things against the God of gods, and shall prosper till the indignation be accomplished: for that that is determined will be done. Neither shall he regard the God of his fathers, nor the desire of women, nor regard any god: for he shall magnify himself above all. But in his estate he shall honor the God of forces: and a god whom his fathers knew not shall he honor with gold, and silver, and with precious stones, and pleasant things.*

This Antichrist kills many believers. See Revelation 6: 9-11 and Rev 7: 9-17.

CHAPTER 8
TECHNOLOGY AND THE RISE OF THE ANTICHRIST

Within the last 25 years we've been immersed – on the brink of being swept away - in a tidal wave of technology - mostly led by the computer industry. We are being revolutionized with technology everyday. As soon as it becomes marketable, it just as quickly becomes obsolete. In this chapter we'll look at some of these new technologies... how they affect us today...where are they leading us...how can they be a tool for the Antichrist.

Is the Recent Explosion of Knowledge a Sign of the Last days?

Daniel 12:4 "But thou Daniel, shut up the words and seal the book, even to the time of the end: many shall run to and fro, **and knowledge shall be increased**."

Consider these figures on the growth of knowledge in our world:

From 1750-1900	250 years	Knowledge doubled
From 1900-1950	50 years	Knowledge doubled
From 1950-1960	10 years	Knowledge doubled
From 1960-1968	8 years	Knowledge doubled
From 1968-1990	every 3 years	Knowledge doubled
From 1990-2001	Every 18 months	Knowledge doubled

Let's look at various technologies in each of the following areas: Internet Super-Highway; Cashless Society; Chip Implants; Government Military; Inventory Control; Global Positioning; Smart Cards, and Biometrics.[3]

---

[3] Excerpts on technology taken from *Final Warning*, Grant Jeffrey, 1995 and *Prince of Darkness*, Grant Jeffrey, 1994.

60 – What's In *Your* Future?

INTERNET SUPER HIGHWAY

The internet has become the new era of communication and accessibility to data. It may surprise you to know that about 25 million young people – not to mention millions more adults - are logged onto the internet everyday. The benefits include having easy access to a world of information; easy communications through email; web cameras to do teleconferencing; search engines for doing research and finding information quickly; online shopping; and much more. However, it also causes a level of isolation and reduces personal communication; it could open children to pornography and other unhealthy distractions; it opens computerized information to terrorist attacks from hackers; chat rooms make children and adults targets for kidnappers and other abuses; and much more.

The internet began as an experiment more than 25 years ago by the Department of Defense Army Research and Planning Agency (ARPA). This agency created a network called ARPAnet, a network to support military research. Eventually ARPAnet grew beyond its expectations and later became known as the Internet. Who runs it? For the most part, **the internet runs itself.** That is, as far as day-to-day operations go. Every organization that is connected to the Internet is simply responsible for its own part. You may be surprised to learn that YOU pay for the Internet. There is a myth that the Internet is free. Someone pays, however, for every connection. Many home users dialing through an Internet Service Provider (ISP) are paying for the service to connect to the Internet, although once connected access to the hosting sites is free.

CASHLESS SOCIETY

We are well on the way to a cashless society: Checking Accounts; Credit Cards; Electronic Bill Paying; Electronic Transfers; and Debit Cards (i.e. the latest and fastest growing - one swipe and immediately your account is debited). Do you use the very convenient EZ PASS system for paying tolls on U.S. highways? If so, when you roll through the toll booth, money is electronically debited immediately from your EZ PASS account. When your account is almost empty, you probably have money electronically transferred from your credit card to your EZ PASS account automatically. It's great for law enforcement because they can track your movement from toll to toll.

In the USA medical studies have shown that cash is a source of disease...

Electronics are also replacing paper in other areas – for example helping to prevent fraud and abuse in the food stamp program...

62 – What's In Your Future?

Electronic Food Stamp card replaces Coupons

"That is the biggest reason why we are pursuing EBT in Missouri," said Melba Price, who oversees the program for the Missouri Department of Social Services. "There is no way in a paper system to get a handle on (the fraud). But when you have an electronic system, you know where every card is being used and how much it is being used for."

The world is already taking the biggest step towards the Mark by becoming accustomed to paperless money.

INVENTORY CONTROL AND TRACKING

It's possible to inventory a warehouse full of items in a matter of minutes rather than days using automation technology…

U.S.A.
New Radio Tags Can Track Product and Person From Distance

A new company was incorporated to commercialize an electronic system developed for the military that can locate and inventory tiny tags on tools, materials, people or equipment at the touch of a button from up to 100 meters away.

The technology is similar to that used in anti-shoplifting tags in stores and in highway toll-booth systems, but the military-grade versions have much greater capabilities, says Ron Gilbert, director of engineering for the firm, Wave ID, Richland, Wash. "These have 10 to 50 times more range and the "interrogator" can simultaneously read 500 tags a second, which is way faster than what is commercially available," he adds.

Gilbert says the signals will penetrate anything except solid metal, allowing a warehouse to be inventoried simply by painting it with a query signal. The tags range in size from that of a grain of rice to a credit card and are expected to cost between 10 cents and $12 depending on sophistication, according to Gilbert.

Total security can only be achieved through total control. The ability to count 500 tags in one second with today's technology may sound mind-boggling, but it's only the beginning.

GLOBAL POSITIONING SYSTEM (GPS)

GPS tracking is a free service. It's owned by the federal government and can find a target as close as 3 feet. Some of our military missiles are GPS / Laser guided. A Global Positioning System device in the car records the position of vehicle every six minutes with satellite technology. The information is radioed back, telling how long the car was in use on any given day and where it went. Trucking companies are already using this technology. The government has requested to the car manufacturers that by the year 2005 every new car must have a GPS tracking ID embedded in the car. The technology already exists. Today, the more expensive cars already come GPS equipped.

Soldier's Meditag Holds 600,000 Pages Of Information

The Pentagon has big plans for a postage-stamp-size semiconductor chip embedded in plastic. Called the Meditag, it could be the dog tag of the 21st century.

Unlike the old-fashioned dog tags worn by soldiers, the Meditag could store 1.2 gigabytes of data - the equivalent of 600,000 single-spaced, typed pages. A soldier's basic medical history, personnel data, fingerprints, or even voice print could be included.

GOVERNMENT MILITARY

The fact that technology continues to surge with exponential momentum, and the threat of world terrorism is rising, one can only surmise that technology will one day soon have the answer to everyone's worries.

The military has been using smart card technology to replace the old dog tags worn by every soldier and airman for identification. Besides name, rank, serial number, and religion, the

64 – What's In Your Future?

new tags can record all the medical history needed by doctors in case of injury.

SMART CARDS

Smart Cards are a little different than the cards most of us have in our wallets. They look the same, except a little thicker. You can hardly notice it. Some of them have contacts in them or use radio waves. Inside the card there is actually a tiny computer.

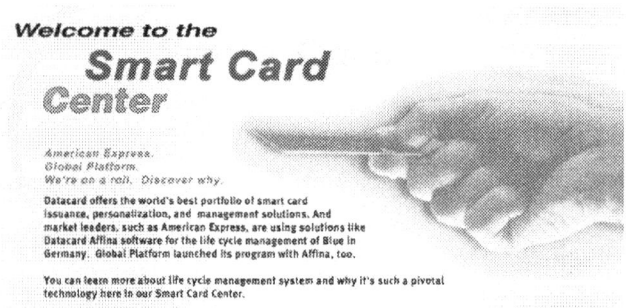

ELECTRONIC IMPLANTS

Today's technology is controlling the movement of millions of animals using microchips the size of a grain of rice, implanted in

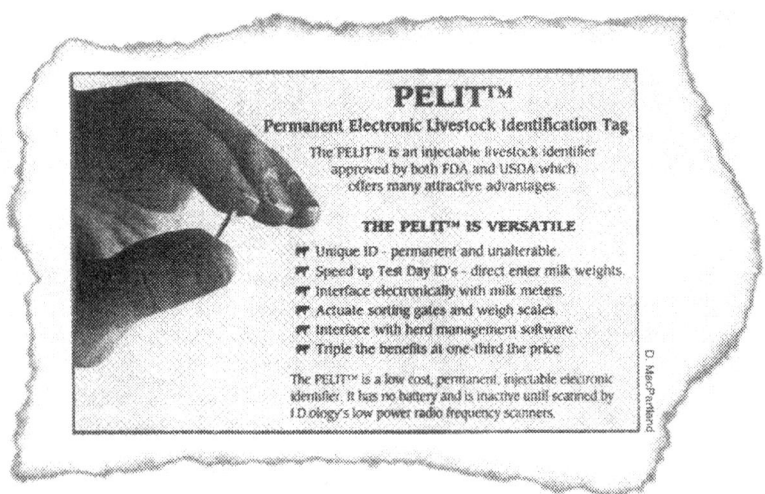

the skin with a small needle and holding information equivalent to

20,000 pages. Canada, USA and the European community are already using it in livestock.

In England, there's a "Body Clock" you can't forget that will remain with you for life.

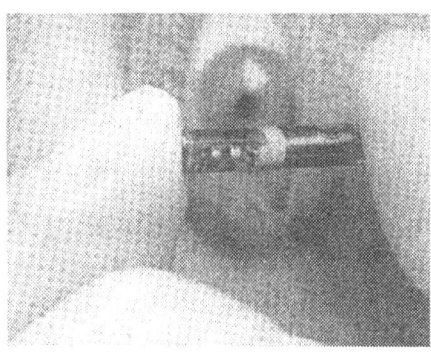

Also in England, Professor Kevin Warwick has become the first person to have a silicon chip implanted in his body. The chip allows computers to communicate directly with his body. He said, "As I walk around the building, lights go on and computers burst into life every time I scratch my head. It can be quite scary." Prof. Warwick's experiment is the first to link machines and mankind in

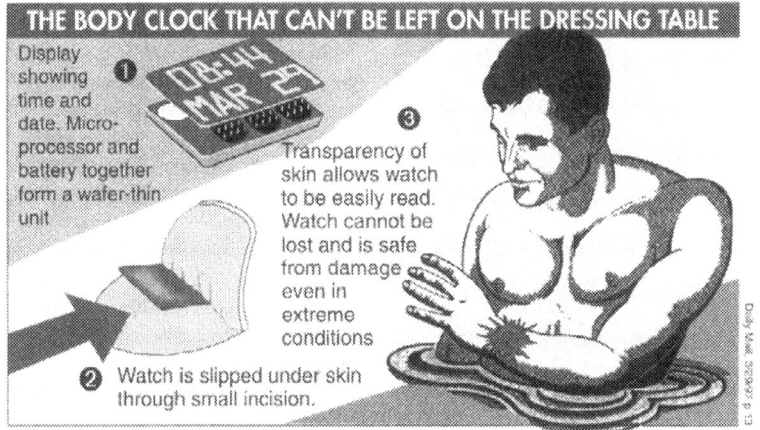

a Faustian pact that could see us controlling our environment simply by our thoughts and movements – or, if it all goes wrong, giving machines the ability to control every aspect of our lives.

A Microchip Implant could replace credit cards, keys, passports, etc. You may one day be fitted with microchip implants that will communicate with your environment. A miniature electronic device contained in a tiny capsule will be implanted in your forearm. It will then send messages to a computer that controls light and heat in intelligent buildings. Such implants could even replace credit cards, keys, passports, and other official documents.

BIOMETRICS

One of the fastest growing technologies today is Biometrics. It is used for deploying security measures both locally and globally. Since the 911 incident, there's been a lot more research in this field and the government is providing financial support for this research. Biometrics are automated methods of recognizing a person based on a physiological or behavioral characteristic. Biometric technologies are becoming the foundation of an extensive array of highly secure identification and personal verification solutions. As the level of security breaches and transaction fraud increases, the need for highly secure identification and personal verification technologies is becoming apparent.

It's being used in many government departments: National Crime Information Center; Immigration and Naturalization Service (INS) passenger accelerated service system; Fingerprint identification system; U.S Department of Justice; Electronic Benefits Transfer; Draft Authentication Module; Federal security infrastructure; and many other federal government operations.

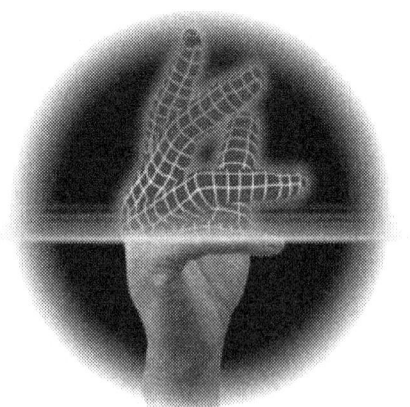

The biometrics being used include: Cornea recognition; Facial recognition; Finger Prints; Vein recognition; and Hand recognition.

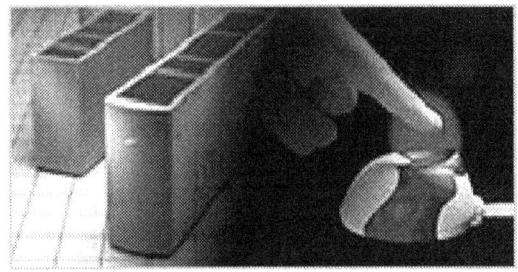

WHERE IS THIS TECHNOLOGY LEADING US?

Not long ago, the government set up a registry on the internet for those individuals who did not want any annoying calls from telemarketers. It was

called the "Do Not Call Registry." Without questioning, 10 million people registered in the first 3 days. Almost 17 million people registered by the third day. Eighty-five percent registered using the Internet. We respond based on "what's in it for me". If it sounds like it will benefit us, then we just do it! But how much of our privacy are we willing to give away?

Are we giving away too much information about ourselves? Today, data is a valued commodity. Every purchase we make is recorded - every contract - every credit decision is being kept in a database repository of personal information. **Who has this data?** Trans Union, TRW/Experian, and CBI/Equifax, the leading credit information bureaus, have more information about us than we ever knew existed. You may not realize it, but any company or organization that you do business with has access to that information. **How much do they know about us?** <u>Everything:</u> How much we earn; how much we spend; what kind of people we are based on statistics and ratings. They know more about us without even knowing <u>who we are</u>.

With the technology that already exists, and with the increase in knowledge in these areas, how then can all this be used by the Antichrist? <u>It's possible that people will accept the chip implant before the Antichrist appears. Then it will be a simple procedure to "identify" who belongs to him and who does not.</u> Implants, combined with other technology, could become commonplace in the world because of problems that the chip will solve : Increased identity theft; Stealing credit cards (if they're around); Kidnapping – the GPS tracking will find lost/kidnapped children/adults; Stolen cars – GPS will track vehicles & drivers with implants; Personal safety - accident identification (e.g. fatal cases); Emergency medical applications & rapid access to records; Military applications (both for fighting wars and for preventing wars by early detection); Buying and selling - we're almost cashless.

Revelation 13:18 indicates that the *"number of the beast"* is 666. It also says that *"it is man's number."* What could this 666 number be? Could it be a literal number? Could it be part of our Social Security Number (SSN)? Could it be a chip implant with a generated number that identifies us with the Antichrist?

Technology and the Rise of the Antichrist -69

Man was created on the sixth day. "6" does not reach perfection. The number "6" is often used as the symbolic number of imperfection of humankind (2 arms, 2 legs, 1 head, 1 body). Man, counterfeiting himself to be like God (i.e. a trinity), could spiritually be symbolized by 666. Here's another possibility using today's technology...

Today, nearly every product we buy from the store has a UPC (Universal Product Code) Symbol called a "bar code". Could the mark of the beast (i.e. the number of the beast) be in a bar code? In 1974, this strange new mark began appearing on products. Until today, virtually every product is now marked with the familiar UPC barcode. And there are three embedded numbers on every UPC. The number "6" starts the code, marks the middle, and ends the code. After doing our own investigation, sure enough they were in every UPC bar code collected. So what does the future hold ?

70 – What's In **Your** Future?

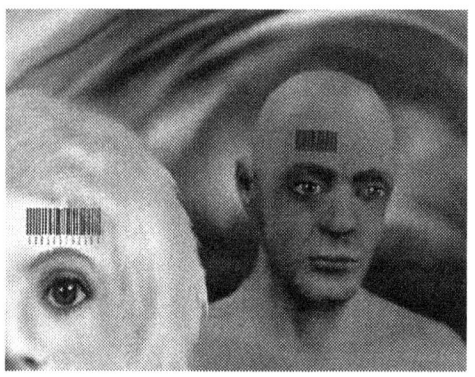

The Antichrist will surely have his own scheme to mark those that accept him. The technology is already available to have his mark implanted in people; use it like a debit card for buying and selling; learn and use information about them; use GPS to track their whereabouts at any time. Inventories of resources (i.e. besides the people themselves) held by various nations can also be tracked and

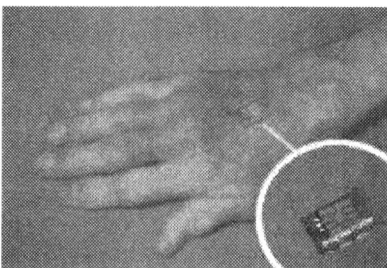

dictatorial decisions made to force money, machines, or other transfers around the world.

Revelation 13:18

[18]Here is wisdom. Let him who has understanding calculate the number of the beast, for it is the number of a man: His number is 666.

King of my life I crown Thee now –
Thine shall the glory be;
Lest I forget Thy thorne-crowned brow,
Lead me to Calvary.
- *Hussey*

CHAPTER 9
THE MARRIAGE SUPPER OF THE LAMB

John now gives us a unique picture of God's throne room. He mentions seven burning lamps, and identifies them as the "seven Spirits of God." This refers to the sevenfold ministry of the one Holy Spirit: rest, wisdom, understanding, counsel, might, knowledge, and fear of God. See Isaiah 11:2. It could also refer to the sevenfold gifts of the Spirit: prophecy, serving, teaching, exhortation, giving, ruling, and mercy. See Romans 12: 6-8.

He also sees what the KJV calls *"beasts"* and the NKJV translates as *"living creatures."* There are four living creatures all representing the work of Christ as our Life: He is the **Lion** of the tribe of Judah. He is the **Calf** (i.e. Lamb) sacrifice of God given for the sins of the world. He humbled Himself and became **Man** and dwelt among us so we could touch and know God intimately. He will return someday like a **Flying Eagle** to snatch away from the earth those who are His.

The six wings could represent that Christ created all life in six days. And the eyes in front and in back tell us that nothing misses His notice. Jesus told us that God sees even a sparrow falling from its nest. Matthew 10:29. He told each of the seven churches in Revelation 2 and 3, *"I know thy works..."* He sees everything and sustains everything. *"And he is before all things and by him all things consist"* (or hold together). Colossians 1:17

The passage begins with lightning and thundering and voices coming from God's throne. Psalm 81: 7 speaks about God answering His people's prayers in a place of "thunder", *"You called in trouble, and I delivered you; I answered you in the secret place of thunder."* Another psalm speaks of the storm that overshadowed Israel as they passed through the Red Sea (Psalm 77:16-20). Its thunder spelled doom for the Egyptians but deliverance for God's people. When Jesus asked His Father to glorify His name in Christ's death (John 12:24-29), God answered from heaven, *"I have both glorified it and will glorify it again."* The crowd only heard what sounded like thunder from heaven. Whenever we're in trouble, and we call to our Father in heaven, we can be sure that He answers us and "thunder" is heard from His throne.

Revelation 4: 5-11

⁵And from the throne proceeded lightnings, thunderings, and voices. Seven lamps of fire were burning before the throne, which are the seven Spirits of God.

⁶Before the throne there was a sea of glass, like crystal. And in the midst of the throne, and around the throne, were four living creatures full of eyes in front and in back. ⁷The first living creature was like a lion, the second living creature like a calf, the third living creature had a face like a man, and the fourth living creature was like a flying eagle. ⁸The four living creatures, each having six wings, were full of eyes around and within. And they do not rest day or night, saying: "Holy, holy, holy, Lord God Almighty, Who was and is and is to come!"

⁹Whenever the living creatures give glory and honor and thanks to Him who sits on the throne, who lives forever and ever, ¹⁰the twenty-four elders fall down before Him who sits on the throne and worship Him who lives forever and ever, and cast their crowns before the throne, saying: ¹¹"You are worthy, O Lord, To receive glory and honor and power; For You created all things, And by Your will they exist and were created."

The Judgment Seat of Christ has caused the Bride of Christ (i.e. all the believers who were raptured and are with Him in Glory) to *"make herself ready"* for the marriage supper of the Lamb. This happens sometime after the Judgment Seat, while the Antichrist and False Prophet are causing lawlessness and havoc on earth, and while God is recovering the earth and pouring out His wrath. It

The Marriage Supper of the Lamb -75

ends sometime just before Christ's return to the Battle of Armageddon. See Appendix A – Biblical Jewish marriage.

Revelation 19:8 says that now *"she was granted (permission) to be arrayed in fine linen, clean and bright, for the fine linen is the righteous acts of the saints."* At the Judgment Seat of Christ, the bride was judged according to what she had done on earth whether good or bad. See 2 Corinthians 5: 10. The things done that were wood, hay, and stubble were burned up. The things that remained were the righteous acts (i.e. gold, silver, and precious stones).

As we shall see later, those who returned on white horses with Christ to Armageddon were *"clothed in fine linen, white and clean."* This is the Bride of Christ riding with Christ to fight for righteousness. See Revelation 19:14.

We don't know the length of time it takes for the marriage supper of the Lamb. It is being presented here because those who will come to Christ during the seven year period of the great tribulation are not part of the marriage supper. They do not have transformed, immortal bodies. They are, however, part of the "first resurrection" and also rule and reign with Christ. See Revelation 20: 4-5. Truly, *"blessed are they who are called to the marriage supper of the Lamb"* (Revelation 19:9).

Revelation 19: 4 - 10

[4] And the twenty-four elders and the four living creatures fell down and worshiped God who sat on the throne, saying, "Amen! Alleluia!" [5] Then a voice came from the throne, saying, "Praise our God, all you His servants and those who fear Him, both small and great!"

[6] And I heard, as it were, the voice of a great multitude, as the sound of many waters and as the sound of mighty thunderings, saying, "Alleluia! For the Lord God Omnipotent reigns! [7] Let us be glad and rejoice and give Him glory, for the marriage of the Lamb has come, and His wife has made herself ready." [8] And to her it was

granted to be arrayed in fine linen, clean and bright, for the fine linen is the righteous acts of the saints.

⁹Then he said to me, "Write: "Blessed are those who are called to the marriage supper of the Lamb!"" And he said to me, "These are the true sayings of God." ¹⁰And I fell at his feet to worship him. But he said to me, "See that you do not do that! I am your fellow servant, and of your brethren who have the testimony of Jesus. Worship God! For the testimony of Jesus is the spirit of prophecy."

CHAPTER 10
GOD'S FINAL CAMPAIGN TO SAVE SOULS AND RECOVER THE EARTH

The key to understanding the events that follow and unlocking the Book of Revelation is found in Genesis 41:25-32. That's where Joseph interpreted Pharaoh's dream. The dream was doubled - but it was one. The fat cows and fat ears of corn told the same story. The lean cows and the lean ears of corn told the same story. The fat cows and the lean cows tell the whole story. The fat ears of corn and the lean ears of corn tell the whole story. Joseph said that God gave it to Pharaoh that way because He would <u>soon bring it to pass</u>.

Similarly, in the Book of Revelation, the seals and angel messengers are telling the same story. The trumpets and the vials are telling the rest of the story. There are different aspects of the story being conveyed by each of the symbols, but the whole story is doubled. The seals and trumpets tell the whole story together, and the angel messengers and the vials tell the whole story together. It's done that way because God says He will bring it to pass quickly – The Lord tells us in the beginning (first verse) and emphasizes in the last chapter that He is revealing to John *"what must shortly come to pass"*. See Rev 1:1, Rev 22: 6,7,12, and 19.

78 – What's In Your Future?

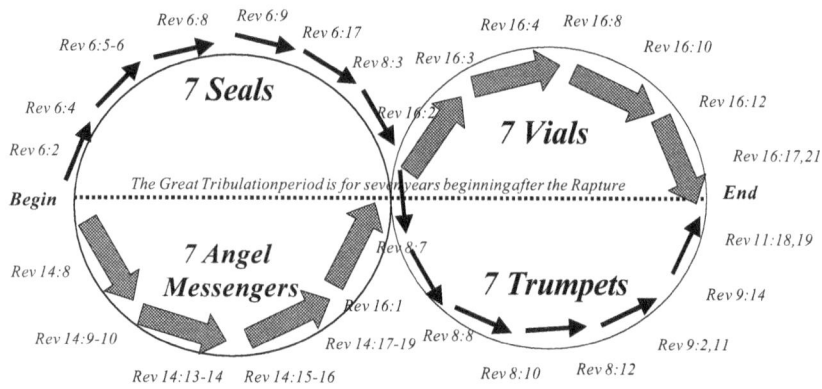

Here's a verse by verse "map" of the double revelation which is really one.

The Book of Revelation consists of this "double prophecy" (i.e. seals/angel messengers and Trumpets/vials) along with various scenes that amplify the prophecy and fill in the missing details.

Here are the various scenes:

The Preserved Jews (7: 1-8)
The Rescued Martyrs (7: 9-17)
The Little Book of Prophecy Eaten (10: 1-11)
The Two Witnesses (11: 1-13)
The Spiritual War in Heaven and On Earth (12: 1-17)
The Two Beasts – Antichrist and False Prophet (13: 1-18 & Daniel 7: 8-14)
The Lamb and the 144,000 (14: 1-5)
The Destruction of Religious Babylon (17: 1-17)
The Destruction of Political Babylon (17: 18 – 18: 24)
The Return of Christ to earth (19: 11-21)

There's another similarity between the Book of Revelation and Joseph's work in Egypt. Joseph's campaign to save lives in Egypt during the seven years of plenty (Genesis 41) is like God's final campaign for the souls of people left behind after the Rapture that we see depicted in the description of the Seals and Angel Messengers. It's also interesting that as the wheat was harvested by Joseph, so in Revelation 14 we see our Lord using harvesting and reaping as a metaphor for taking from the earth those who are His and have eternal life. We'll discuss this in the next chapter.

As the next scene unfolds, John hears an angel ask who is worthy to open a scroll – to open its seals. Jesus, as The Lamb of God, is declared to be worthy to open the seals. The scene is similar to a last will and testament being probated with all the parties receiving what the deceased declared would be theirs. Jesus gave His life for the sins of the world, and is therefore worthy to unseal the will and declare what the world will now receive.

Revelation 5: 1-14

¹ And I saw in the right hand of Him who sat on the throne a scroll written inside and on the back, sealed with seven seals. ²Then I saw a strong angel proclaiming with a loud voice, "Who is worthy to open the scroll and to loose its seals?" ³And no one in heaven or on the earth or under the earth was able to open the scroll, or to look at it.

⁴So I wept much, because no one was found worthy to open and read the scroll, or to look at it. ⁵But one of the elders said to me, "Do not weep. Behold, the Lion of the tribe of Judah, the Root of David, has prevailed to open the scroll and to loose its seven seals."

⁶And I looked, and behold, in the midst of the throne and of the four living creatures, and in the midst of the elders, stood a Lamb as though it had been slain, having seven horns and seven eyes, which are the seven Spirits of God sent out into all the earth. ⁷Then He came and took the scroll out of the right hand of Him who sat on the throne.

⁸Now when He had taken the scroll, the four living creatures and the twenty-four elders fell down before the Lamb, each having a

harp, and golden bowls full of incense, which are the prayers of the saints. ⁹And they sang a new song, saying: "You are worthy to take the scroll, And to open its seals; For You were slain, And have redeemed us to God by Your blood Out of every tribe and tongue and people and nation, ¹⁰And have made us kings and priests to our God; And we shall reign on the earth."

¹¹Then I looked, and I heard the voice of many angels around the throne, the living creatures, and the elders; and the number of them was ten thousand times ten thousand, and thousands of thousands, ¹²saying with a loud voice: "Worthy is the Lamb who was slain To receive power and riches and wisdom, And strength and honor and glory and blessing!"

¹³And every creature which is in heaven and on the earth and under the earth and such as are in the sea, and all that are in them, I heard saying: "Blessing and honor and glory and power Be to Him who sits on the throne, And to the Lamb, forever and ever!"

¹⁴Then the four living creatures said, "Amen!" And the twenty-four elders fell down and worshiped Him who lives forever and ever.

MORE INFORMATION FROM SCRIPTURE

Jeremiah 30: 5-7 – **Jacob's trouble**. *"This is what the LORD says: 'Cries of fear are heard-- terror, not peace. Ask and see: Can a man bear children? Then why do I see every strong man with his hands on his stomach like a woman in labor, every face turned deathly pale? How awful that day will be! None will be like it. It will be a time of trouble for Jacob, but he will be saved out of it.'"*

Zechariah 13: 8-9 and Ezekiel 36: 24-28 – **2/3 of Jews on earth die and the remainder become the Lord's.**

Zechariah 13: 8-9 – '*In the whole land,' declares the LORD, 'two-thirds will be struck down and perish; yet one-third will be left in it. This third I will bring into the fire; I will refine them like silver and test them like gold. They will call on my name and I will answer them; I will say, 'They are my people,' and they will say, 'The LORD is our God'.*"

Ezekiel 36: 24-28 "'*For I will take you out of the nations; I will gather you from all the countries and bring you back into your own land. I will sprinkle clean water on you, and you will be clean; I will cleanse you from all your impurities and from all your idols. I will give you a new heart and put a new spirit in you; I will remove from you your heart of stone and give you a heart of flesh. And I will put my Spirit in you and move you to follow my decrees and be careful to keep my laws. You will live in the land I gave your forefathers; you will be my people, and I will be your God.*'"

Sift the substance of my life,
Filter out the sin and strife;
Leave me, Lord, a purer soul,
Cleansed and sanctified and whole.
- Lemon

CHAPTER 11
THE SEALS AND ANGEL MESSENGERS

The seals and angel messengers when read together as different accounts of the same event reveal God's final campaign to spread the Gospel and then reap the earth – to gather His own unto himself – and to cast the others into the winepress of His wrath.

FIRST SEAL OPENED AND FIRST ANGEL MESSENGER

After the first seal is removed, we see a rider on a white horse with a bow (See 2 Kings 13:17) who goes forth conquering and to conquer. Horses represent swiftness. So this event will happen quickly. White stands for purity – the purity of the Word of God and the gospel message. God wants that none should perish (John 3: 16), and so He gives those left behind after the rapture a final chance to accept Christ as Savior and Lord. However, unlike the rider on the white horse in Revelation 19, this rider has limited power because the campaign for souls lasts a short time.

Revelation 6: 1-2

[1] Now I saw when the Lamb opened one of the seals; and I heard one of the four living creatures saying with a voice like thunder, "Come and see." [2] And I looked, and behold, a white horse. He who sat on it had a bow; and a crown was given to him, and he went out conquering and to conquer.

John sees an angel messenger who has the everlasting gospel to preach to every nation, kindred, tongue, and people – "fear God and give Him glory for the hour of judgment has come." He's saying that their time to waiver about choosing Christ has run out. It's now or never! As God reserved 7000 who had not bowed to Baal and whose mouths had not kissed him (1 Kings19: 18), He has a remnant who will not prostitute themselves by worshipping the Beast.

Revelation 14: 6-7

⁶Then I saw another angel flying in the midst of heaven, having the everlasting gospel to preach to those who dwell on the earth--to every nation, tribe, tongue, and people-- ⁷saying with a loud voice, "Fear God and give glory to Him, for the hour of His judgment has come; and worship Him who made heaven and earth, the sea and springs of water."

Revelation 12: 10-12

¹⁰Then I heard a loud voice saying in heaven, "Now salvation, and strength, and the kingdom of our God, and the power of His Christ have come, for the accuser of our brethren, who accused them before our God day and night, has been cast down. ¹¹<u>And they overcame him by the blood of the Lamb and by the word of their testimony, and they did not love their lives to the death.</u> ¹²Therefore rejoice, O heavens, and you who dwell in them! Woe to the inhabitants of the earth and the sea! For the devil has come down to you, having great wrath, because he knows that he has a short time."

Revelation 11: 1-2

¹ Then I was given a reed like a measuring rod. And the angel stood, saying, "Rise and measure the temple of God, the altar, and those who worship there. ²But leave out the court which is outside the temple, and do not measure it, for it has been given to the Gentiles. And they will tread the holy city underfoot for forty-two months.

God's great grace is shown even now. He has prepared people to witness to those left behind. The number given in Revelation is two. That is the number of "confirmation" (i.e. one witnesses and the other confirms). They may represent two classes of witnesses. He says that they are lampstands and olive trees. The lampstands, we've seen earlier stand for the church (i.e. Gentiles who are left behind but come to believe in Christ). The olive trees probably represent Jewish believers since the olive tree was given as a symbol of Israel. See Jeremiah 11:16, Romans 11:24.

If there are actually just two witnesses rather than classes of witnesses, they would most likely be Enoch and Elijah. They were taken to heaven without dying. See Genesis 5:23 and 2 Kings 2:11. Revelation 11:7 tells us that they are eventually killed – which would fulfill Hebrews 9:27 that says that a person can only die once. In the case of Elijah, James 5:17 declares that he was a man just like other men, and that he prayed and God stopped it from raining for 3 ½ years – similar to what these witnesses can do! Elijah could represent the circumcised believers (i.e. Jews), and Enoch represent the uncircumcised believers (i.e. Gentiles).

Oil comes from olive trees. This is the oil used to light the lampstands. These symbols also say that these witnesses have wisdom, light, and the power (unction) of the Holy Spirit. They speak to people but they are standing before God – that means they are ready for action. They are more than witnesses. They are prophets. A true witness is forced to speak the things he has seen and heard. And a prophet speaks with such force that many hate it. He can't avoid making many enemies. Remember how Jesus said Jerusalem was the place that killed the prophets – so the ministry of these witnesses as prophets will bring them into conflict with the religious system (and the False Prophet) of the tribulation period and eventually martyrdom.

Revelation 11: 3-6

[3] And I will give power to my two witnesses, and they will prophesy one thousand two hundred and sixty days, clothed in sackcloth."

[4] These are the two olive trees and the two lampstands standing before the God of the earth. [5] And if anyone wants to harm them, fire proceeds from their mouth and devours their enemies. And if anyone wants to harm them, he must be killed in this manner.

⁶These have power to shut heaven, so that no rain falls in the days of their prophecy; and they have power over waters to turn them to blood, and to strike the earth with all plagues, as often as they desire.

SECOND SEAL OPENED AND SECOND ANGEL MESSENGER

When the second seal is opened, John sees a red horse and a rider that was given a great sword with power to take peace from the earth. Jesus told us that He came to bring a division and a sword – not peace. Luke 12:51. He said that some day members of the same family would be enemies because of Him. Some will think they were doing God's will by killing other family members. Luke 21: 16, John 16:2. The Apostle Paul identified The Word of God as the sword of the Spirit. Ephesians 6: 17.

Revelation 6: 3-4

³When He opened the second seal, I heard the second living creature saying, "Come and see." ⁴Another horse, fiery red, went out. And it was granted to the one who sat on it to take peace from the earth, and that people should kill one another; and there was given to him a great sword.

Babylon represents the place where idol worship began – where all evil conduct has its source – all spiritual prostitution and abominations. She's called the mother of harlots and abomination of the earth. Revelation 17: 5. She's the habitation of devils and every foul spirit. Revelation 18: 2. Christ warned the churches, earlier in the Book, not to tolerate this kind of behavior. The Lord commands those who are His, *"come out of her my people…"* Revelation 18: 4. Because people dwell in spiritual Babylon, they don't accept the Gospel message, the shed blood of Christ, or the sword of the Spirit. So they ambush each other. There can be no peace with God or with one another in this place.

When the angel says, *"Babylon is fallen",* it's like our saying today that because of Christ sin has no power over us. In the

Spirit, God proclaims that it is done! She is defeated by the Word of God.

Revelation 14: 8

⁸And another angel followed, saying, "Babylon is fallen, is fallen, that great city, because she has made all nations drink of the wine of the wrath of her fornication."

THIRD SEAL OPENED AND THIRD ANGEL MESSENGER

John sees a black horse and a rider with a pair of balances. He hears the high price for the staples of life. There's a high price to pay for physical survival at this time. This scene also represents God's judgment coming. As Daniel 5: 27 describes the Babylonian empire being weighed in the scales and found wanting, so also God's judgment upon unbelievers will be administered quickly.

Revelation 6: 5-6

⁵When He opened the third seal, I heard the third living creature say, "Come and see." So I looked, and behold, a black horse, and he who sat on it had a pair of scales in his hand. ⁶And I heard a voice in the midst of the four living creatures saying, "A quart of wheat for a denarius, and three quarts of barley for a denarius; and do not harm the oil and the wine."

The high cost for believing in Christ is death. People will either worship the beast, and get his mark to allow them to buy and sell, or accept Christ and die. Inhabitants of the earth at this time must choose between living physically a short time, and going through God's wrath and eternal death, or dying physically and enjoying eternal life with Christ.

Revelation 14: 9-12

⁹Then a third angel followed them, saying with a loud voice, "If anyone worships the beast and his image, and receives his mark on his forehead or on his hand, ¹⁰he himself shall also drink of the wine of the wrath of God, which is poured out full strength into the cup of His indignation. He shall be tormented with fire and brimstone in the presence of the holy angels and in the presence of the Lamb. ¹¹And the smoke of their torment ascends forever and ever; and they have no rest day or night, who worship the beast and his image, and whoever receives the mark of his name."

¹²Here is the patience of the saints; here are those who keep the commandments of God and the faith of Jesus.

FOURTH SEAL OPENED AND FOURTH ANGEL MESSENGER

John sees a pale horse next. The rider is Death and Hell (Hades) is following him. This rider is given power to kill one quarter of the earth's inhabitants. The word translated Hell could also be translated "grave" (as in 1 Corinthians 15:22). Some die because of the tribulation from God. Others die because they accept Christ as Savior and are beheaded. Later, we see these under the altar in heaven.

Revelation 6: 7-8

⁷When He opened the fourth seal, I heard the voice of the fourth living creature saying, "Come and see." ⁸So I looked, and behold, a pale horse. And the name of him who sat on it was Death, and Hades followed with him. And power was given to them over a fourth of the earth, to kill with sword, with hunger, with death, and by the beasts of the earth.

Those who die because of their belief in Christ are blessed. In deed, under the persecution from the Antichrist at this time, death is a blessing because the Lord is getting ready to reap the earth of those who are His. Many will literally have their *physical* heads cut off to make Christ their "head" as the Church does *in the Spirit* today. These believers will escape the wrath of God coming soon upon the earth.

Here's a poem that expresses very well the blessing of death in Christ. Though officially the author is unknown, I believe it was written by Joanie Yoder after the death of her husband. Joanie is now safely home with the Lord herself…

SAFELY HOME

I am home in Heaven, dear ones – Oh, so happy and so bright
There is perfect joy and beauty, in this everlasting light.
All the pain and grief are over, every restless tossing passed.
I am now at peace forever, safely home in Heaven at last.
Did you wonder I so calmly trod the valley of the Shade?
Oh, but Jesus' love illuminated every dark and fearful glade.
And He came Himself to meet me in the way so hard to tread;
And with Jesus' arm to lean on, could I have one doubt or dread?
Then you must not grieve so sorely, for I love you dearly still.
Try to look beyond death's shadows; pray to trust our Father's will.
There is work still waiting for you. So you must not idly stand.
Do it now while life remaineth; you shall rest in Jesus' hand.
When that work is all completed, He will gently call you home.
Oh, the rapture of that meeting – Oh, the joy to see you come.

Revelation 14: 13-14

[13]Then I heard a voice from heaven saying to me, "Write: "Blessed are the dead who die in the Lord from now on."' "Yes," says the Spirit, "that they may rest from their labors, and their works follow them."

[14]Then I looked, and behold, a white cloud, and on the cloud sat One like the Son of Man, having on His head a golden crown, and in His hand a sharp sickle.

This is something Jesus spoke about in the parable of the wheat and the tares…

> *Matthew 13:24-30 "Another parable put he forth unto them saying, The kingdom of heaven is likened unto a man which sowed good seed in his field; But while men slept, his enemies came and sowed tares among the wheat, and went his way. But when the blade was sprung, and brought forth fruit, then appeared the tares also. So the servants of the householder came and said to him, Sir, didst not thou sow good seed in thy field? From whence then hath it tares? He said unto them, An enemy hath done this. The servants said unto him, Wilt thou then that we go and gather them up? But he said, Nay; lest while ye gather up the tares, ye root up the wheat with them.* <u>*Let both grow together until the harvest; and in the time of the harvest I will say to the reapers, Gather ye together first the tares, and bind them in bundles to burn them: but gather the wheat into my barn.*</u>*"*

FIFTH SEAL OPENED AND FIFTH ANGEL MESSENGER

The next scene shows souls "under the altar". They are people who have been killed on earth because they believed the gospel message and witnessed to others about Christ.

Revelation 6: 9-11

[9] When He opened the fifth seal, I saw under the altar the souls of those who had been slain for the word of God and for the testimony which they held. [10] And they cried with a loud voice, saying, "How long, O Lord, holy and true, until You judge and avenge our blood on those who dwell on the earth?" [11] Then a white robe was given to each of them; and it was said to them that they should rest a little while longer, until both the number of their fellow servants and their brethren, who would be killed as they were, was completed.

God's two witnesses have been proclaiming the gospel message for about 3 ½ years. As mentioned earlier, the ministry of God's witnesses during the tribulation period end in martyrdom. Jerusalem killed God's prophets. That's where these witnesses are killed. Jerusalem is called Sodom and Egypt because it had become seat of the Beast with her spiritual prostitution and corruption. It stands for the false religious system of the Tribulation. If you have a prophet's ministry in the church today, don't be surprised if you are exposed to shame and ridicule in the streets of Jerusalem – the church.

Not only were their bodies left unburied, but the unbelievers of earth were rejoicing because of it. They were sending each other gifts, having parties, and rejoicing because these prophets had tormented them. Please don't forget, however, that their testimony for 3 ½ years has won many souls for Christ also. The gospel has done its work to divide the sheep from the goats.

Their bodies were left unburied for 3 ½ days. Then the Lord (in essence) said, *"That's enough for you – come home my servants."* They are raised from the dead and "reaped" from the earth by our Lord Jesus Christ along with others who have believed.

Revelation 11:7-14

[7]When they finish their testimony, the beast that ascends out of the bottomless pit will make war against them, overcome them, and kill them. [8]And their dead bodies will lie in the street of the great city which spiritually is called Sodom and Egypt, where also our Lord was crucified. [9]Then those from the peoples, tribes, tongues, and nations will see their dead bodies three-and-a-half days, and not allow their dead bodies to be put into graves. [10]And those who dwell on the earth will rejoice over them, make merry, and send gifts to one another, because these two prophets tormented those who dwell on the earth.

[11]Now after the three-and-a-half days the breath of life from God entered them, and they stood on their feet, and great fear fell on

those who saw them. ¹²And they heard a loud voice from heaven saying to them, "Come up here." And they ascended to heaven in a cloud, and their enemies saw them. ¹³In the same hour there was a great earthquake, and a tenth of the city fell. In the earthquake seven thousand people were killed, and the rest were afraid and gave glory to the God of heaven. ¹⁴The second woe is past. Behold, the third woe is coming quickly.

Here is the Lord shown actually reaping those souls who are His from the earth. From Revelation 6: 9-11 that we just read, these are put *"under the altar"* – a place of waiting in the presence of the Lord.

Revelation 14: 15-16

¹⁵And another angel came out of the temple, crying with a loud voice to Him who sat on the cloud, "Thrust in Your sickle and reap, for the time has come for You to reap, for the harvest of the earth is ripe." ¹⁶So He who sat on the cloud thrust in His sickle on the earth, and the earth was reaped.

After Christ reaps the earth, His attention turns to a special remnant of Jews. The Lord orders they be sealed to protect them from the coming wrath of God through the trumpets and vials over the next 3 ½ years. They are 144,000 in number equally divided among the twelve tribes. We see them in Revelation 14: 1-5 on Mount Zion with Christ the Lamb. They have *"kept themselves pure"* and were the *"first fruits to God and the Lamb."* This refers to their being redeemed (i.e. purchased by Christ's blood) – probably the first Jews of this period to recognize Christ as Messiah. They are probably used by God to give their testimony, evangelize, and help other Jews prepare to receive Christ as Messiah. See Revelation 12 above.

Revelation 7: 1-8

¹ After these things I saw four angels standing at the four corners of the earth, holding the four winds of the earth, that the wind

should not blow on the earth, on the sea, or on any tree. ²Then I saw another angel ascending from the east, having the seal of the living God. And he cried with a loud voice to the four angels to whom it was granted to harm the earth and the sea, ³saying, "Do not harm the earth, the sea, or the trees till we have sealed the servants of our God on their foreheads." ⁴And I heard the number of those who were sealed. One hundred and forty-four thousand of all the tribes of the children of Israel were sealed:

⁵of the tribe of Judah twelve thousand were sealed;
of the tribe of Reuben twelve thousand were sealed;
of the tribe of Gad twelve thousand were sealed;
⁶of the tribe of Asher twelve thousand were sealed;
of the tribe of Naphtali twelve thousand were sealed;
of the tribe of Manasseh twelve thousand were sealed;
⁷of the tribe of Simeon twelve thousand were sealed;
of the tribe of Levi twelve thousand were sealed;
of the tribe of Issachar twelve thousand were sealed;
⁸of the tribe of Zebulun twelve thousand were sealed;
of the tribe of Joseph twelve thousand were sealed;
of the tribe of Benjamin twelve thousand were sealed.

John now sees all those who have believed the gospel message and escaped God's wrath (i.e. the "great tribulation) by accepting Jesus as Savior and Lord – "reaped" by Christ. They are standing before the throne of God in heaven. *"Standing before the throne"* means that they are ready to serve the Lord in any way He requires.

Revelation 7: 9-17

⁹After these things I looked, and behold, a great multitude which no one could number, of all nations, tribes, peoples, and tongues, standing before the throne and before the Lamb, clothed with white robes, with palm branches in their hands, ¹⁰and crying out with a loud voice, saying, "Salvation belongs to our God who sits on the throne, and to the Lamb!" ¹¹All the angels stood around the throne and the elders and the four living creatures, and fell on their faces before the throne and worshiped God, ¹²saying: "Amen! Blessing

and glory and wisdom, Thanksgiving and honor and power and might, Be to our God forever and ever. Amen."

[13] Then one of the elders answered, saying to me, "Who are these arrayed in white robes, and where did they come from?" [14] And I said to him, "Sir, you know."

So he said to me, "These are the ones who come out of the great tribulation, and washed their robes and made them white in the blood of the Lamb. [15] Therefore they are before the throne of God, and serve Him day and night in His temple. And He who sits on the throne will dwell among them. [16] They shall neither hunger anymore nor thirst anymore; the sun shall not strike them, nor any heat; [17] for the Lamb who is in the midst of the throne will shepherd them and lead them to living fountains of waters. And God will wipe away every tear from their eyes."

SIXTH SEAL OPENED AND SIXTH ANGEL MESSENGER

With those who accepted Christ having been reaped, and the special remnant of Jews sealed, the great day of God's wrath upon people and nations will no longer be delayed. God sends a great earthquake and a shaking of the solar system. People seek death but are denied.

Revelation 6:12-17

[12] I looked when He opened the sixth seal, and behold, there was a great earthquake; and the sun became black as sackcloth of hair, and the moon became like blood. [13] And the stars of heaven fell to the earth, as a fig tree drops its late figs when it is shaken by a mighty wind. [14] Then the sky receded as a scroll when it is rolled up, and every mountain and island was moved out of its place. [15] And the kings of the earth, the great men, the rich men, the commanders, the mighty men, every slave and every free man, hid themselves in the caves and in the rocks of the mountains, [16] and said to the mountains and rocks, "Fall on us and hide us from the face of Him who sits on the throne and from the wrath of the

Lamb! ¹⁷For the great day of His wrath has come, and who is able to stand?"

As God's wrath begins, an angel reaps unbelievers and casts them into a winepress that symbolizes God's crushing blows – It's called *"the winepress of the wrath of God"* - about to strike the unrepentant.

Revelation 14:17-20

¹⁷Then another angel came out of the temple which is in heaven, he also having a sharp sickle.

¹⁸And another angel came out from the altar, who had power over fire, and he cried with a loud cry to him who had the sharp sickle, saying, "Thrust in your sharp sickle and gather the clusters of the vine of the earth, for her grapes are fully ripe." ¹⁹So the angel thrust his sickle into the earth and gathered the vine of the earth, and threw it into the great winepress of the wrath of God. ²⁰And the winepress was trampled outside the city, and blood came out of the winepress, up to the horses' bridles, for one thousand six hundred furlongs.

SEVENTH SEAL OPENED AND SEVENTH ANGEL MESSENGER

The verses that follow describe how angels begin getting ready to administer God's wrath. The specific punishments are executed by angels with seven trumpets and seven vials that follow in the next chapter.

Revelation 8:1-6

¹ When He opened the seventh seal, there was silence in heaven for about half an hour. ²And I saw the seven angels who stand before God, and to them were given seven trumpets. ³Then another angel, having a golden censer, came and stood at the altar. He was given much incense, that he should offer it with the prayers of all the saints upon the golden altar which was before the throne. ⁴And

the smoke of the incense, with the prayers of the saints, ascended before God from the angel's hand. ⁵Then the angel took the censer, filled it with fire from the altar, and threw it to the earth. And there were noises, thunderings, lightnings, and an earthquake. ⁶So the seven angels who had the seven trumpets prepared themselves to sound.

Revelation 15:1-8

¹ Then I saw another sign in heaven, great and marvelous: seven angels having the seven last plagues, for in them the wrath of God is complete.

²And I saw something like a sea of glass mingled with fire, and those who have the victory over the beast, over his image and over his mark and over the number of his name, standing on the sea of glass, having harps of God. ³They sing the song of Moses, the servant of God, and the song of the Lamb, saying: "Great and marvelous are Your works, Lord God Almighty! Just and true are Your ways, O King of the saints! ⁴Who shall not fear You, O Lord, and glorify Your name? For You alone are holy. For all nations shall come and worship before You, For Your judgments have been manifested."

⁵After these things I looked, and behold, the temple of the tabernacle of the testimony in heaven was opened. ⁶And out of the temple came the seven angels having the seven plagues, clothed in pure bright linen, and having their chests girded with golden bands. ⁷Then one of the four living creatures gave to the seven angels seven golden bowls full of the wrath of God who lives forever and ever. ⁸The temple was filled with smoke from the glory of God and from His power, and no one was able to enter the temple till the seven plagues of the seven angels were completed.

Revelation 16:1

[1] Then I heard a loud voice from the temple saying to the seven angels, "Go and pour out the bowls of the wrath of God on the earth."

God dwells in light and holiness,
In splendor and in might;
And godly fear of His great power
Can help us do what's right.
- D. De Haan

CHAPTER 12
THE TRUMPETS AND THE VIALS

The unparalleled trouble that follows serves to punish the unbelieving nations and restore Israel to spiritual favor. The Seven Trumpets and the Seven Vials describe God's specific wrath being poured out on unbelievers using the earth, sea, rivers and fountains of waters, sun, Euphrates River, the "seat of the beast", and a great plague of hail. The time between the different disasters is unknown. We believe, however, that they are completed in 31/2 years, climaxing with the return of Christ.

This is the last half of Daniel's seventieth "seven", described in Daniel 9: 24-27. The angel Gabriel told Daniel, *"Seventy 'sevens' (i.e. 70 weeks of years or 490 years) are decreed for your people and your holy city to finish transgression, to put an end to sin, to atone for wickedness, to bring in everlasting righteousness, to seal up vision and prophecy and to anoint the most holy."* Clearly, this scripture is speaking about bringing an end to all unrighteousness and anointing Christ as Messiah and King of kings at His second coming. Also see Revelation 11:15. The 490 years would begin from *"the issuing of the decree to restore and rebuild Jerusalem"* (verse 25).

There are various explanations for these 490 years. We think that Fred G. Zaspel[4] provides good insight. God had "issued His word" to Jeremiah in 587 B.C. promising the end of Israel's captivity and the rebuilding of Jerusalem (Jeremiah 32:1, 6-9, 13-17, 24-27). There cannot possibly be any *"decree to restore and rebuild Jerusalem"* any more significant than His. Daniel 9: 25 (ASV) then says, *"...from the going forth of the word to restore and build Jerusalem to the coming of an anointed one, a prince, there shall be seven weeks. Then for sixty-two weeks it shall be built again with squares and moat, but in a troubled time."* When we read "an anointed one, a prince" or "messiah prince" we generally think

---

[4] Daniel's "Seventy Weeks", An Historical and Exegetical Analysis, 1991

immediately of Jesus Christ, the Messiah. But the Scriptures are not so restrictive (e.g., 1 Samuel 2:10, Hannah of the King; 1 Samuel 16:6, Samuel of Eliab; 1 Samuel 24:6, David of Saul; etc.). Most significantly, God Himself calls Cyrus "His anointed" (Isaiah 45:1). This is significant, for Cyrus was one who would not even "know" the Lord (Isaiah 45:4). In his remarkable prophecy Isaiah predicts the arrival of "Cyrus" who will be the deliverer of Israel; as such he would be "God's anointed."

It seems, then, that the seven sevens began in 587 B.C. with God's word to Jeremiah concerning the rebuilding of Jerusalem and ended in 538 B.C. with Cyrus' decree to end Jewish captivity.

> 587 B.C. (God's word to Jeremiah)
> +<u>49</u> years (7 X 7)
> 538 B.C. ("an anointed one, a prince"- Cyrus)

Verse 26 says, *"After sixty-two 'sevens' (i.e. 434 years) the anointed one will be cut off."* A starting point is not specified for the sixty-two sevens, but verse 26 states that *"after the sixty two sevens Messiah shall be cut off."* Given that this is a reference to the crucifixion of Jesus Christ, the sixty-two sevens must run out prior to that time. Notice it is "after" the sixty-two sevens that Messiah is cut off. Zaspel concludes that Nehemiah's rebuilding of Jerusalem is the starting point for the 62 sevens and Christ's birth is the end point.

The question is whether the 490 years were to be considered consecutive or rather if unspecified gaps were involved. Since verse 25 makes a clear distinction between the seven sevens and the sixty-two sevens, could their separation signify a "time-gap" between them? This would not be at all unusual in Biblical prophecy (e.g., Daniel.11:2-3; Micah 5:1-2), and there is nothing to indicate that such a "gap" between the first seven and the next sixty-two sevens would constitute any violation of the text. In fact, a gap between these two periods is the only explanation available to account for their separation. Assuming gaps are allowed, then the beginning of these sixty-two weeks seems to be Nehemiah's rebuilding of Jerusalem. Nehemiah's request to Artaxerxes to return to the city was in April, 444 B.C. (Nehemiah.2:1). According to Josephus,[5] Nehemiah went first to Babylon to find volunteers among the Jews to return with him. With this and the various preparations involved and the obtaining of building materials (which is probable, since his rebuilding began soon after his arrival in Jerusalem), his actual arrival in Jerusalem would have taken some time, probably several years. Josephus puts it at "the twenty-fifth year" of Artaxerxes - 440 B.C.

    440 B.C. (The beginning of the rebuilding in times of distress)
    +<u>434</u> years (62 X 7)
    6 B.C. (Birth of Christ)

This verse then speaks about a prince coming who will *"destroy the city and the sanctuary. The end will come like a flood: War will continue until the end, and desolations have been determined."* This same ruler *"will confirm a covenant with many for one 'seven' (i.e. 7 years)."* This period we believe refers to the 7 years of tribulation after the rapture of believers. For some reason, perhaps His will that none should perish, the Lord has determined to delay the coming of the last 'seven'- and so there's another unspecified gap of time in this prophecy.

This *"coming prince,"* is Paul's *"man of lawlessness"* and John's *"beast from the sea"* whose activities are in "immediate" proximity to the return of Jesus Christ (Matthew. 24:29; 2 Thessalonians. 2:3ff; Revelation 19:11-20:3). See Appendix A. It would seem that he is also the "antichrist" of 1 John 4:3. His activities will continue *"even until the end, and until that which is decreed shall be poured out upon the desolator."* That is, at the "end" of the final seven he will be destroyed.

"In the middle of the seven (i.e. after 3 ½ years) he (i.e. the ruler – Antichrist) will put an end to sacrifice and offering. And on a wing

---

[5] *Antiquities,* XI, V, 7

of the temple will set up an abomination that causes desolation, until the end that is decreed is poured out on him (verse 27)."* In Matthew 24:15-21, Jesus spoke of this *"abomination of desolation"*. He said, *"So when you see standing in the holy place 'the abomination that causes desolation' spoken of through the prophet Daniel...then let those who are in Judea flee to the mountains...For then there will be distress (the KJV says 'great tribulation') unequaled from the beginning of the world until now – and never to be equaled again."* So it seems clear that the Antichrist setting up his image in the temple to be worshipped after breaking his covenant with Israel and others will be met by God pouring out His wrath upon the earth.

THE FIRST TRUMPET SOUNDS AND THE FIRST VIAL IS POURED OUT

The first trumpet and vial are executed upon the earth. A sore is inflicted on man and blood, mixed with fire and hail, rains down. Everywhere man turns he is choked by the smoke from the burning all around him.

Revelation 8:7

[7] The first angel sounded: And hail and fire followed, mingled with blood, and they were thrown to the earth. And a third of the trees were burned up, and all green grass was burned up.

Revelation 16:2

[2] So the first went and poured out his bowl upon the earth, and a foul and loathsome sore came upon the men who had the mark of the beast and those who worshiped his image.

SECOND TRUMPET SOUNDS AND SECOND VIAL IS POURED OUT

The next disasters are executed upon the sea in two stages. God sends a great mountain crashing into the sea. It probably creates a huge tsunami that destroys one-third of all ships and living creatures (including man). In a second blow from God, the sea turns to blood and all living creatures in the sea are destroyed.

Revelation 8: 8-9

⁸Then the second angel sounded: And something like a great mountain burning with fire was thrown into the sea, and a third of the sea became blood. ⁹And a third of the living creatures in the sea died, and a third of the ships were destroyed.

Revelation 16:3

³Then the second angel poured out his bowl on the sea, and it became blood as of a dead man; and every living creature in the sea died.

THIRD TRUMPET SOUNDS AND THIRD VIAL IS POURED OUT

The third disasters are executed upon the rivers and fountains of waters. First, something like a meteorite falls from heaven and poisons the waters so that many people die. Then God turns these rivers and other drinking systems into blood – like the blood man took from God's prophets and others He sent to them.

Revelation 8:10-11

¹⁰Then the third angel sounded: And a great star fell from heaven, burning like a torch, and it fell on a third of the rivers and on the springs of water. ¹¹The name of the star is Wormwood. A third of the waters became wormwood, and many men died from the water, because it was made bitter.

Revelation 16: 4-7

⁴Then the third angel poured out his bowl on the rivers and springs of water, and they became blood. ⁵And I heard the angel of

the waters saying: "You are righteous, O Lord, The One who is and who was and who is to be, Because You have judged these things. ⁶For they have shed the blood of saints and prophets, And You have given them blood to drink. For it is their just due."

⁷And I heard another from the altar saying, "Even so, Lord God Almighty, true and righteous are Your judgments."

FOURTH TRUMPET SOUNDS AND FOURTH VIAL IS POURED OUT

The sun, moon, and stars are targeted for the next set of disasters. At first, a third of the day and also a third of the night is without light. That essential element for growth of any plant that's left is partially taken away. We can also assume that it is much colder all over the world. Then, God reverses the torment and causes the sun to scorch man with great heat. Still man doesn't repent.

Revelation 8:12-13

¹²Then the fourth angel sounded: And a third of the sun was struck, a third of the moon, and a third of the stars, so that a third of them were darkened. A third of the day did not shine, and likewise the night.

¹³And I looked, and I heard an angel flying through the midst of heaven, saying with a loud voice, "Woe, woe, woe to the inhabitants of the earth, because of the remaining blasts of the trumpet of the three angels who are about to sound!"

Revelation 16: 8-9

⁸Then the fourth angel poured out his bowl on the sun, and power was given to him to scorch men with fire. ⁹And men were scorched with great heat, and they blasphemed the name of God who has power over these plagues; and they did not repent and give Him glory.

FIFTH TRUMPET SOUNDS AND FIFTH VIAL IS POURED OUT

When the fifth angel sounds and the fifth angel pours out his vial, John is drawn to what's called the "bottomless pit" and the "seat of the beast." The bottomless pit is later heard in Revelation 20:1. It's where Satan will be chained for 1000 years. In fact, it's in Hell where he has his current base of operations. Since Satan gives the Antichrist (i.e. the beast) his power, the "seat of the beast" could be Satan's headquarters. It could also mean the location where the Antichrist takes up his headquarters in Jerusalem.

John sees smoke from the bottomless pit that darkens the sun and the air. This is very much like we think of Hell (i.e. that place of separation from God and continual torment). As the description unfolds, however, the Lord may be describing something else. John sees locusts coming out of this furnace, whose wings sound like *"chariots of many horses running into battle",* and which have armored breastplates. Their tails and their stings were like scorpions. These "locusts" didn't eat the grass or other plants like ordinary locusts. Instead they tormented man for five months – which brought man to the point of desiring death, but it didn't come. The attributes ascribed to these locusts sound very much like an underground missile silo – perhaps with many small missiles carrying chemical weapons.

Scorpions are venomous arthropods. There's about 1300 species worldwide. They are characterized by an elongated body and a segmented tail that is tipped with a venomous stinger. The venom contains complex mixtures of neurotoxins (i.e. poisons that affect the nervous system). The U.S. species has venom that produces severe pain and swelling at the site of the sting, numbness, frothing at the mouth, difficulties in breathing, muscle twitching, and convulsions.[6]

The Desert Locust is one of about a dozen species of short-horned grasshoppers that are known to change their behavior and form swarms of adults or bands of hoppers (wingless nymphs). The swarms that form can be dense and highly mobile. During plagues, Desert Locusts may spread over an enormous area of some 17.5 million square miles, extending over or into parts of 60 countries. This is more than 20% of the total land surface of the world. During plagues, the Desert Locust has the potential to damage the livelihood of a tenth of the world's population. Locust swarms can vary from a little more than ½ mile to several hundred square miles. There can be at least 40 million and sometimes as many as 80 million locust adults in each .6 mile of swarm.[7]

What John saw may exist now or be developed in future years. They probably filled the sky like millions of locusts so they could reach every part of the earth to torment all those who had the mark of the beast.

The instrument God used to produce all this torment upon man is called in Hebrew Abaddon and in Greek called Apollyon. These words mean "Destroyer." He is said to be the *"angel of the bottomless pit"* (i.e. Satan). He may have "poisoned" the minds of the Antichrist or other world leaders to show their strength, gain dominion, and bring other nations to their knees. Remember, the kingdom of Antichrist is made up of ten toes of iron and clay – substances that don't mix!

Revelation 9: 1-12
[1] Then the fifth angel sounded: And I saw a star fallen from heaven to the earth. To him was given the key to the bottomless pit. [2] And he opened the bottomless pit, and smoke arose out of the pit like the smoke of a great furnace. So the sun and the air were

---

[6] Desert USA, www.desertusa.com/Oct96/du_scorpion.html
[7] Desert Locust Information Service, www.fao.org/news/global/locusts

darkened because of the smoke of the pit. ³Then out of the smoke locusts came upon the earth. And to them was given power, as the scorpions of the earth have power. ⁴They were commanded not to harm the grass of the earth, or any green thing, or any tree, but only those men who do not have the seal of God on their foreheads. ⁵And they were not given authority to kill them, but to torment them for five months. Their torment was like the torment of a scorpion when it strikes a man. ⁶In those days men will seek death and will not find it; they will desire to die, and death will flee from them.

⁷The shape of the locusts was like horses prepared for battle. On their heads were crowns of something like gold, and their faces were like the faces of men. ⁸They had hair like women's hair, and their teeth were like lions' teeth. ⁹And they had breastplates like breastplates of iron, and the sound of their wings was like the sound of chariots with many horses running into battle. ¹⁰They had tails like scorpions, and there were stings in their tails. Their power was to hurt men five months. ¹¹And they had as king over them the angel of the bottomless pit, whose name in Hebrew is Abaddon, but in Greek he has the name Apollyon.

¹²One woe is past. Behold, still two more woes are coming after these things.

Revelation 16:10-11

¹⁰Then the fifth angel poured out his bowl on the throne of the beast, and his kingdom became full of darkness; and they gnawed their tongues because of the pain. ¹¹They blasphemed the God of heaven because of their pains and their sores, and did not repent of their deeds.

SIXTH TRUMPET SOUNDS AND SIXTH VIAL IS POURED OUT

The sixth set of disasters is executed on the *"great river Euphrates."* John sees the spirits of devils drawing the kings of the earth into a great battle – *"the battle of that great day of God Almighty."* This is the Battle of Armageddon. The river Euphrates is dried up to make way for the *"kings of the east."*

The army is said to be made up of two hundred million "horsemen." The "horses" are said to have heads like lions that issue fire, smoke, and brimstone from their mouths that kill people. They also have tails which were like snakes with heads that also cause damage. Their breastplates were fiery red, dark blue, and yellow as sulfur.

What sounds a lot like thousands of horses going to battle? Armored tanks traveling along the desert floor sound like many horses. We even say that tanks have so much "horse power." The front of a tank-like vehicle has what looks like a large head. The cannon or a modified cannon could be considered a *"mouth that issues fire, smoke, and brimstone."* It can also be equipped with a machine gun (snake-like) turret or some smaller weapon system in the "tail" end. This end would have a smaller head-like shape for the machine gun.

Tank systems that are available today fire laser-guided munitions on precise targets. They can fire about 7 rounds a minute and hit targets about 15 miles away. They can probably be equipped with local nuclear weapons. With this kind of fire power, and with many nations engaged in battle with millions of troops, *"a third part of mankind was killed by the fire and the smoke and the brimstone."*

Revelation 9:13-21

[13]Then the sixth angel sounded: And I heard a voice from the four horns of the golden altar which is before God, [14]saying to the sixth angel who had the trumpet, "Release the four angels who are

bound at the great river Euphrates." ¹⁵So the four angels, who had been prepared for the hour and day and month and year, were released to kill a third of mankind. ¹⁶Now the number of the army of the horsemen was two hundred million; I heard the number of them. ¹⁷And thus I saw the horses in the vision: those who sat on them had breastplates of fiery red, hyacinth blue, and sulfur yellow; and the heads of the horses were like the heads of lions; and out of their mouths came fire, smoke, and brimstone. ¹⁸By these three plagues a third of mankind was killed--by the fire and the smoke and the brimstone which came out of their mouths. ¹⁹For their power is in their mouth and in their tails; for their tails are like serpents, having heads; and with them they do harm.

²⁰But the rest of mankind, who were not killed by these plagues, did not repent of the works of their hands, that they should not worship demons, and idols of gold, silver, brass, stone, and wood, which can neither see nor hear nor walk. ²¹And they did not repent of their murders or their sorceries or their sexual immorality or their thefts.

Revelation 16:12-16

¹²Then the sixth angel poured out his bowl on the great river Euphrates, and its water was dried up, so that the way of the kings from the east might be prepared. ¹³And I saw three unclean spirits like frogs coming out of the mouth of the dragon, out of the mouth of the beast, and out of the mouth of the false prophet. ¹⁴For they are spirits of demons, performing signs, which go out to the kings of the earth and of the whole world, to gather them to the battle of that great day of God Almighty.

¹⁵"Behold, I am coming as a thief. Blessed is he who watches, and keeps his garments, lest he walk naked and they see his shame."

¹⁶And they gathered them together to the place called in Hebrew, Armageddon.

John is asked to eat a scroll in the hand of a mighty angel. It is this Book of Revelation. Figuratively, John is to fill himself up with the book so he can then "feed" others with its message. It is a bitter sweet experience for John. It is "sweet" to be used of the Lord to give the truth to others but it is "bitter" because of the persecution to the messenger that it brings. It will also be "sweet" for those who will hear the message and search for its hidden delicacies, but it will be "bitter" for those who will not obey its message. This incident with John is reminiscent and similar to the prophet Ezekiel's experience of eating another scroll in Ezekiel 2: 9 – 3:4.

The mighty angel declares there will be no more delay in executing God's orders for wrath and His final victory.

Revelation 10: 1-11

¹ I saw still another mighty angel coming down from heaven, clothed with a cloud. And a rainbow was on his head, his face was like the sun, and his feet like pillars of fire. ²He had a little book open in his hand. And he set his right foot on the sea and his left foot on the land, ³and cried with a loud voice, as when a lion roars. When he cried out, seven thunders uttered their voices. ⁴Now when the seven thunders uttered their voices, I was about to write; but I heard a voice from heaven saying to me, "Seal up the things which the seven thunders uttered, and do not write them."

⁵The angel whom I saw standing on the sea and on the land raised up his hand to heaven ⁶and swore by Him who lives forever and ever, who created heaven and the things that are in it, the earth and the things that are in it, and the sea and the things that are in it, that there should be delay no longer, ⁷but in the days of the sounding of the seventh angel, when he is about to sound, the mystery of God would be finished, as He declared to His servants the prophets.

⁸Then the voice which I heard from heaven spoke to me again and said, "Go, take the little book which is open in the hand of the angel who stands on the sea and on the earth."

⁹So I went to the angel and said to him, "Give me the little book." And he said to me, "Take and eat it; and it will make your stomach bitter, but it will be as sweet as honey in your mouth."

¹⁰Then I took the little book out of the angel's hand and ate it, and it was as sweet as honey in my mouth. But when I had eaten it, my stomach became bitter. ¹¹And he said to me, "You must prophesy again about many peoples, nations, tongues, and kings."

An angel with one of the seven vials now describes God's judgment against a prostitute riding on the back of a scarlet colored beast. The prostitute represents spiritual Babylon. The Antichrist kingdom is only the personification of Babylon which has existed over all the past millennia. There is a religious (Chapter 17) and political (Chapter 18) Babylon. On her forehead is written "Mystery Babylon the Great – Mother of Harlots." In Chapter 17, she represents all the false religions since the city of Babel, where spiritual prostitution started. She's dressed like a prostitute who is trying to solicit herself to men. She's being carried along by the same beast of Chapter 12 – Satan. To understand this fully, we need to look at some history beginning in Babel (i.e. Babylon).

In the city of Babel, Nimrod wanted to start a one world religion. He built a tower to worship the sun (the source of life), moon, stars, and other celestial bodies. See Genesis 11. Nimrod means "rebel." It is said of Nimrod that he was a great warrior and mighty hunter. See Genesis 10:9-10. This was meant, however, in the sense that he rebelled against God and hunted men to join his rebellion. This is what the prostitute (Mystery Babylon) is doing in Revelation 17.

Spiritual adultery started in Babylon. Nimrod's wife, Semirimis, took on the title of "Queen of Heaven." She was a witch of Satan. And when Nimrod died, she convinced his followers that he had become a ray of the sun (the source of life) and had miraculously impregnated her with a son, Tommuz. She also convinced them later that Tommuz had died and come back to life again. So Tommuz became the counterfeit resurrected son of God, who was one with his father. This religion spread to many parts of the world after God confounded man's language, so they couldn't understand one another, and scattered them. See Genesis 11:1-9. We find the Queen of Heaven being worshipped by the people of Israel in Jeremiah 44:17, 25.

Nimrod was also the first leader to establish a monarchy. His rule over several tribes apparently comes through power of conquest and not because he is their natural patriarchal head. Nimrod established Babylon (from the city of Babel), and later the city of Nineveh. See Genesis 10: 9-10. He wanted one world government with its headquarters in Babel (Genesis 11: 3-4). This is the Babylon we see in Revelation 18 in which the kings of the earth live deliciously (verse 9). It's where the merchants and those who live and work by the sea have prospered greatly. Today, in the 21st century, we call it a "global economy." In this political Babylon, the lust for money and materialism is rampant. And it's where grabbing power, prestige, political influence, and every other evil use and dominion over people resides. See verses 9-19.

Revelation 17: 8-11 refers to a beast carrying the prostitute. Verse 8 is a reference to Satan, who "was" (i.e. accepted as Lucifer, an angel of God), "is not" (i.e. an enemy of God – as good as dead), and who "will ascend out of the bottomless pit" (i.e. will get one more chance before destruction after Christ's 1000-year reign). Verse 9 refers to seven hills (i.e. "seven mountains") that the woman sits upon. This could be reference to the entire world (i.e. seven continents), but is more likely (since seven kings are mentioned) the seven kingdoms of Revelation 12. Verse 10 says five are fallen – Egypt, Assyria, Babylon, Media-Persia, Greco-Macedonia; one is – Rome; and one that had not yet come but when it does will be short-lived - the Antichrist kingdom. Verse 11 mentions an eighth kingdom, referring to Satan's kingdom of deceit and darkness.

Revelation 17:1-18

¹ Then one of the seven angels who had the seven bowls came and talked with me, saying to me, "Come, I will show you the judgment of the great harlot who sits on many waters, ²with whom the kings of the earth committed fornication, and the inhabitants of the earth were made drunk with the wine of her fornication."

³So he carried me away in the Spirit into the wilderness. And I saw a woman sitting on a scarlet beast which was full of names of blasphemy, having seven heads and ten horns. ⁴The woman was arrayed in purple and scarlet, and adorned with gold and precious stones and pearls, having in her hand a golden cup full of abominations and the filthiness of her fornication. ⁵And on her forehead a name was written:
   MYSTERY, BABYLON THE GREAT, THE MOTHER OF HARLOTS AND OF THE ABOMINATIONS OF THE EARTH.

⁶I saw the woman, drunk with the blood of the saints and with the blood of the martyrs of Jesus. And when I saw her, I marveled with great amazement. ⁷But the angel said to me, "Why did you marvel? I will tell you the mystery of the woman and of the beast that carries her, which has the seven heads and the ten horns. ⁸The beast that you saw was, and is not, and will ascend out of the bottomless pit and go to perdition. And those who dwell on the earth will marvel, whose names are not written in the Book of Life from the foundation of the world, when they see the beast that was, and is not, and yet is.

⁹"Here is the mind which has wisdom: The seven heads are seven mountains on which the woman sits. ¹⁰There are also seven kings. Five have fallen, one is, and the other has not yet come. And when he comes, he must continue a short time. ¹¹The beast that was, and is not, is himself also the eighth, and is of the seven, and is going to perdition.

¹²"The ten horns which you saw are ten kings who have received no kingdom as yet, but they receive authority for one hour as kings with the beast. ¹³These are of one mind, and they will give their power and authority to the beast. ¹⁴These will make war with the Lamb, and the Lamb will overcome them, for He is Lord of lords and King of kings; and those who are with Him are called, chosen, and faithful."

¹⁵Then he said to me, "The waters which you saw, where the harlot sits, are peoples, multitudes, nations, and tongues. ¹⁶And the ten horns which you saw on the beast, these will hate the harlot, make her desolate and naked, eat her flesh and burn her with fire. ¹⁷For God has put it into their hearts to fulfill His purpose, to be of one mind, and to give their kingdom to the beast, until the words of God are fulfilled. ¹⁸And the woman whom you saw is that great city which reigns over the kings of the earth."

Revelation 18:1-19

¹ After these things I saw another angel coming down from heaven, having great authority, and the earth was illuminated with his glory. ²And he cried mightily with a loud voice, saying, "Babylon the great is fallen, is fallen, and has become a dwelling place of demons, a prison for every foul spirit, and a cage for every unclean and hated bird! ³For all the nations have drunk of the wine of the wrath of her fornication, the kings of the earth have committed fornication with her, and the merchants of the earth have become rich through the abundance of her luxury."

⁴And I heard another voice from heaven saying, "Come out of her, my people, lest you share in her sins, and lest you receive of her plagues. ⁵For her sins have reached to heaven, and God has remembered her iniquities. ⁶Render to her just as she rendered to you, and repay her double according to her works; in the cup which she has mixed, mix double for her. ⁷In the measure that she glorified herself and lived luxuriously, in the same measure give her torment and sorrow; for she says in her heart, "I sit as queen, and am no widow, and will not see sorrow.' ⁸Therefore her plagues

will come in one day--death and mourning and famine. And she will be utterly burned with fire, for strong is the Lord God who judges her.

[9]"The kings of the earth who committed fornication and lived luxuriously with her will weep and lament for her, when they see the smoke of her burning, [10]standing at a distance for fear of her torment, saying, "Alas, alas, that great city Babylon, that mighty city! For in one hour your judgment has come.'

[11]"And the merchants of the earth will weep and mourn over her, for no one buys their merchandise anymore: [12]merchandise of gold and silver, precious stones and pearls, fine linen and purple, silk and scarlet, every kind of citron wood, every kind of object of ivory, every kind of object of most precious wood, bronze, iron, and marble; [13]and cinnamon and incense, fragrant oil and frankincense, wine and oil, fine flour and wheat, cattle and sheep, horses and chariots, and bodies and souls of men. [14]The fruit that your soul longed for has gone from you, and all the things which are rich and splendid have gone from you, and you shall find them no more at all. [15]The merchants of these things, who became rich by her, will stand at a distance for fear of her torment, weeping and wailing, [16]and saying, "Alas, alas, that great city that was clothed in fine linen, purple, and scarlet, and adorned with gold and precious stones and pearls! [17]For in one hour such great riches came to nothing.' Every shipmaster, all who travel by ship, sailors, and as many as trade on the sea, stood at a distance [18]and cried out when they saw the smoke of her burning, saying, "What is like this great city?'

[19]"They threw dust on their heads and cried out, weeping and wailing, and saying, "Alas, alas, that great city, in which all who had ships on the sea became rich by her wealth! For in one hour she is made desolate.'

As verse 21 begins, we see a mighty angel take up a great stone and cast it into the sea. He says this is the way Babylon will be thrown down. It reminds us of Nebuchadnezzar's dream in which a stone is cut from a mountain without human hands and is cast at the Antichrist kingdom of ten toes of iron and clay. Daniel says this means that the stone will consume all the other kingdoms and the God of heaven will set up a kingdom that shall never be destroyed (i.e. Christ's second coming and His kingdom). See Daniel 2:36-45.

Revelation 18: 20-24

^{20}"Rejoice over her, O heaven, and you holy apostles and prophets, for God has avenged you on her!"

^{21}Then a mighty angel took up a stone like a great millstone and threw it into the sea, saying, "Thus with violence the great city Babylon shall be thrown down, and shall not be found anymore. ^{22}The sound of harpists, musicians, flutists, and trumpeters shall not be heard in you anymore. No craftsman of any craft shall be found in you anymore, and the sound of a millstone shall not be heard in you anymore. ^{23}The light of a lamp shall not shine in you anymore, and the voice of bridegroom and bride shall not be heard in you anymore. For your merchants were the great men of the earth, for by your sorcery all the nations were deceived. ^{24}And in her was found the blood of prophets and saints, and of all who were slain on the earth."

SEVENTH TRUMPET SOUNDS AND SEVENTH VIAL IS POURED OUT

The seventh disaster that befalls earth begins by declaring a great victory for Christ and His people – that the kingdoms of the world have become the kingdoms of our Lord and His Christ, and that He shall rule forever. This victory is affirmed by the temple being opened, the ark of God's promises being revealed, God's voice thundering the command. On earth there's a plague of hail weighing 100 pounds each, and also the biggest earthquake of all time.

The earthquake causes one tenth of Jerusalem to fall with seven thousand people there being killed. The rest became so afraid that they gave glory to God. The city is divided into three parts. This seems to be a continuing part of the Battle of Armageddon. Zechariah 14: 3-4 says, *"Then the LORD will go out and fight against those nations, as he fights in the day of battle. On that day his feet will stand on the Mount of Olives, east of Jerusalem, and the Mount of Olives will be split in two from east to west, forming a great valley, with half of the mountain moving north and half moving south."*

Revelation 11:15-19

[15] Then the seventh angel sounded: And there were loud voices in heaven, saying, "The kingdoms of this world have become the kingdoms of our Lord and of His Christ, and He shall reign forever and ever!" [16] And the twenty-four elders who sat before God on their thrones fell on their faces and worshiped God, [17] saying: "We give You thanks, O Lord God Almighty, The One who is and who was and who is to come, Because You have taken Your great power and reigned. [18] The nations were angry, and Your wrath has come, And the time of the dead, that they should be judged, And that You should reward Your servants the prophets and the saints, And those who fear Your name, small and great, And should destroy those who destroy the earth."

[19] Then the temple of God was opened in heaven, and the ark of His covenant was seen in His temple. And there were lightnings, noises, thunderings, an earthquake, <u>and great hail</u>.

Revelation 16:17-21

[17] Then the seventh angel poured out his bowl into the air, and a loud voice came out of the temple of heaven, from the throne, saying, "It is done!" [18] And there were noises and thunderings and lightnings; and there was a great earthquake, such a mighty and great earthquake as had not occurred since men were on the earth.

¹⁹Now the great city was divided into three parts, and the cities of the nations fell. And great Babylon was remembered before God, to give her the cup of the wine of the fierceness of His wrath. ²⁰Then every island fled away, and the mountains were not found. <u>²¹And great hail from heaven fell upon men, each hailstone about the weight of a talent. Men blasphemed God because of the plague of the hail, since that plague was exceedingly great.</u>

Revelation 19:1-3

¹ After these things I heard a loud voice of a great multitude in heaven, saying, "Alleluia! Salvation and glory and honor and power belong to the Lord our God! ²For true and righteous are His judgments, because He has judged the great harlot who corrupted the earth with her fornication; and He has avenged on her the blood of His servants shed by her." ³Again they said, "Alleluia! Her smoke rises up forever and ever!"

CHAPTER 13
THE BATTLE OF ARMAGEDDON

Christ returns with His saints to recover the earth and set up world rule.

After the marriage supper of the Lamb, the bride was granted that *"she be arrayed in fine linen, clean and bright, for the fine linen is the righteous acts of the saints."* Knowing our Lord, He will serve us at that banquet – as much as we will want to serve Him, then as now, we shall never be able to "out give" the Lord.

And immediately after this wondrous "love feast", we swiftly find ourselves ready for battle – the final battle for righteousness! John sees heaven opened (Revelation 19: 11-21) and Christ, with many crowns (i.e. those we cast at His feet – Revelation 4:10), is seated upon a white horse. His name is called Faithful and True, the Word of God. On His thigh is written, KING OF KINGS and LORD OF LORDS. Revelation 19: 16. And all the redeemed saints, described as *"the armies in heaven clothed in fine linen, white and clean"*, follow Him on white horses back to earth for the battle of Armageddon. John records that he saw the beast (i.e. Antichrist) and the kings of the earth, and their armies gathered together to make war against Him that sat on the horse and His army. Revelation 19: 19.

Every eye shall see Him and His entourage. We will be all aglow, shining like stars, (Daniel 12:3) with the Sun of Righteousness leading us. We'll look like billions of smaller lights flowing behind Him forming His mantle. Then, what God told Abraham, Isaac, and Jacob about their descendents being as innumerable as the stars of heaven will become literally true. Remember His words to Abraham, *"Look now toward heaven, and tell the stars, if thou be able to number them: and he said unto him, So shall thy seed be."* (Genesis 15:5).

Revelation 19:15 then says, *"And out of his mouth goeth a sharp sword, that with it he should smite the nations: and he shall rule them with a rod of iron: and he treadeth the winepress of the fierceness and wrath of Almighty God."* He casts the Antichrist and the false prophet into the lake of fire burning with brimstone. And Satan is chained up. Our Lord will then separate the nations as He describes in Matthew 25:31-46 and His thousand-year reign begins on earth with us ruling and reigning with Him.

Christ's return and His using the saints to rule and reign on the earth have some similarities to Pharaoh using Joseph to reign over Egypt. Genesis 41:37-45. After Joseph interpreted his dream, Pharaoh made Joseph a king (i.e. second only to himself) but also made him a servant to Egypt. We will be both rulers and servants with Christ on the earth. Revelation 5:10, 20:6. *"I hereby put you (i.e. Joseph) in charge of the whole land of Egypt."* Genesis 41:40. This is like Revelation 20:4 where Christ gives His people thrones and authority to judge. *"He dressed him (i.e. Joseph) in robes of fine linen..."* (41:42) - like Christ's saints are dressed in Revelation 19:14. *"...and put a gold chain around his (i.e. Joseph's) neck."* (41:42) - like Christ giving His saints eternal light in their foreheads (Daniel 12:3, Revelation 22:4). *"He had him (i.e. Joseph) ride in a chariot as his second-in-command..."* (41:43) - like Christ giving His saints white horses to ride (Revelation 19:14). And Pharaoh gave Joseph a new name (41:45) - as Christ will give His saints (Revelation 2:17, 3:12).

The return of Christ at Armageddon has been compared with the Battle of Ezekiel 38 and 39. There are different opinions – some believe they are one and the same – others disagree. Here's a comparison to help you decide.

The Battle of Armageddon -121

Comparison Of Great Russian War With Battle of Armageddon

RUSSIAN WAR (Ezekiel 38 & 39)

- Israel living safely – vs 11
- Russia wants material gain – vs 4,12
- Battle is in mountains – vs 8
- Led by Gog – vs 2,7
- Russia and some allies – vs 1-7
- Nation against nation – Ez 38-39
- The defeat comes from natural events and infighting – vs 19-21.
- It ends with the defeat of Russia and its allies – Ez 39

BATTLE OF ARMAGEDDON (Rev)

- Jews live in fear of antichrist – 12:6
- Nations drawn by 3 unclean spirits – 16:13-14
- Battle starts in Meggido plains -16:16
- Led by Antichrist – 19:19
- Seems like more nations – 16:14
- Nations against Christ – 19:19
- Defeat comes by Christ's return – 19:21
  - But Ez 38:20 – "...and all the people on the face of the earth will tremble at my presence".
- It ends with coming of Christ – Rev 19.
  - But see Ez 39:29 – "I will no longer hide my face from them, for I will pour out my Spirit on the house of Israel..."
  - Zech 13:6 "What are these wounds in thine hands? And he shall answer, 'Those with which I was wounded in the house of my friends.'"

Some people believe Ezekiel 38-39 refers to the battle after the thousand year reign of Christ on earth because of Rev 20:8 – *"And shall go out to deceive the nations which are in the four quarters of the earth, Gog and Magog, to gather them together to battle..."*

Revelation 19:11-14

¹¹Now I saw heaven opened, and behold, a white horse. And He who sat on him was called Faithful and True, and in righteousness He judges and makes war. ¹²His eyes were like a flame of fire, and on His head were many crowns. He had a name written that no one knew except Himself. ¹³He was clothed with a robe dipped in blood, and His name is called The Word of God. ¹⁴And the armies in heaven, clothed in fine linen, white and clean, followed Him on white horses.

Revelation 1:7

⁷Behold, He is coming with clouds, and every eye will see Him, even they who pierced Him. And all the tribes of the earth will mourn because of Him. Even so, Amen.

MORE INFORMATION FROM SCRIPTURE

Daniel 12:3. **The returning saints will be shinning like stars – with Mt of Transfiguration light.** *"And they that be wise shall shine as the brightness of the firmament; and they that turn many to righteousness as the stars for ever and ever."*

Genesis 15:5-6. **The returning saints will be like the stars Abraham saw.** *"And he (God) brought him (Abraham) forth abroad, and said, Look now toward heaven, and tell the stars, if thou be able to number them: and he said unto him, So shall they seed be. And he believed in the Lord: and he counted it to him for righteousness."*

Zechariah 13:6. **The people who crucified Christ (i.e. the Jews) will see His wounds when He returns.** *"And one shall say unto him, 'What are these wounds in your hands?' And he shall answer, 'Those with which I was wounded in the house of my friends.'"*

The sword (i.e. the spoken word) that proceeds out of Christ's mouth is two-edged. It can bring life or kill. He spoke the word and His friend Lazarus, who was dead four days, came to life again. John 11:38-44. In a short while (Revelation 20:4) Christ will resurrect those who were beheaded for their testimony of Christ, who did not receive the mark of the Beast. We are told about Christ, *"In the beginning was the Word, and the Word was with God, and the Word was God. He was with God in the beginning. Through him all things were made; without him nothing was made that has been made. In him was life…"* John 1:1-4. As Alpha and Omega, He is the beginning and ending of life itself. In the verses that follow, we see the other edge of that sword as Christ's word brings death. He also orders that the Beast and False Prophet be cast into the lake of fire.

Revelation 19:15-21

[15]Now out of His mouth goes a sharp sword, that with it He should strike the nations. And He Himself will rule them with a rod of iron. He Himself treads the winepress of the fierceness and wrath

of Almighty God. ¹⁶And He has on His robe and on His thigh a name written: KING OF KINGS AND LORD OF LORDS.

¹⁷Then I saw an angel standing in the sun; and he cried with a loud voice, saying to all the birds that fly in the midst of heaven, "Come and gather together for the supper of the great God, ¹⁸that you may eat the flesh of kings, the flesh of captains, the flesh of mighty men, the flesh of horses and of those who sit on them, and the flesh of all people, free and slave, both small and great."

¹⁹And I saw the beast, the kings of the earth, and their armies, gathered together to make war against Him who sat on the horse and against His army. ²⁰Then the beast was captured, and with him the false prophet who worked signs in his presence, by which he deceived those who received the mark of the beast and those who worshiped his image. These two were cast alive into the lake of fire burning with brimstone. ²¹And the rest were killed with the sword which proceeded from the mouth of Him who sat on the horse. And all the birds were filled with their flesh.

The Lord also orders that Satan be chained up where he cannot influence anyone for 1000 years. Life will go on without the devil's deceit or his temptations to defy God's authority or commit idolatry by worshipping other gods.

Revelation 20:1-3

¹ Then I saw an angel coming down from heaven, having the key to the bottomless pit and a great chain in his hand. ²He laid hold of the dragon, that serpent of old, who is the Devil and Satan, and bound him for a thousand years; ³and he cast him into the bottomless pit, and shut him up, and set a seal on him, so that he should deceive the nations no more till the thousand years were finished. But after these things he must be released for a little while.

MORE INFORMATION FROM SCRIPTURE

Daniel 11: 44 – **The Antichrist is opposed from the North and East.** *"But reports from the east and the north will alarm him, and he will set out in a great rage to destroy and annihilate many."*

Zechariah 14: 1-2 – **The fighting reaches Jerusalem, and the Jews there suffer horribly.** *"A day of the LORD is coming when your plunder will be divided among you. I will gather all the nations to Jerusalem to fight against it; the city will be captured, the houses ransacked, and the women raped. Half of the city will go into exile, but the rest of the people will not be taken from the city."*

Zechariah 14: 3-9 – **When all seems hopeless, Jesus (with the saints) descends to the Mount of Olives.** *"Then the LORD will go out and fight against those nations, as he fights in the day of battle. On that day his feet will stand on the Mount of Olives, east of Jerusalem, and the Mount of Olives will be split in two from east to west, forming a great valley, with half of the mountain moving north and half moving south. You will flee by my mountain valley, for it will extend to Azel. You will flee as you fled from the earthquake in the days of Uzziah king of Judah. Then the LORD my God will come, and all the holy ones with him. On that day there will be no light, no cold or frost. It will be a unique day, without daytime or nighttime--a day known to the LORD. When evening comes, there will be light. On that day living water will flow out from Jerusalem, half to the eastern sea and half to the western sea, in summer and in winter. The LORD will be king over the whole earth. On that day there will be one LORD, and his name the only name."*

Zechariah 12: 6-9 – **The Jews are given strength.** *"On that day I will make the leaders of Judah like a firepot in a woodpile, like a flaming torch among sheaves. They will consume right and left all the surrounding peoples, but Jerusalem will remain intact in her place. The LORD will save the dwellings of Judah first, so that the honor of the house of David and of Jerusalem's inhabitants* *may not be greater than that of Judah. On that day the LORD will shield those who live in Jerusalem, so that the feeblest among them will be like David, and the house of David will be like God, like the Angel of the LORD going before them. On that day I will set out to destroy all the nations that attack Jerusalem."*

Zechariah 14: 12, 15 – **The Lord sends a plague on His enemies and some animals**. *"This is the plague with which the LORD will strike all the nations that fought against Jerusalem: Their flesh will rot while they are still standing on their feet, their eyes will rot in their sockets, and their tongues will rot in their mouths. A similar plague will strike the horses and mules, the camels and donkeys, and all the animals in those camps."*

In the secret of His presence
How my soul delights to hide!
Oh, how precious are the lessons
Which I learn at Jesus' side!
- *Goreh*

CHAPTER 14
RULING AND REIGNING WITH CHRIST 1000 YEARS

Have you ever watched what the winner of a race does just after running through the finish line? If it's an Olympic contest, with many nations represented, there always seems to be someone prepared to hand the winner his nation's flag so he/she can carry it around the track in victory. They have "center-stage". For a brief moment in history, the winner seems to be at the center of the universe. All alone now, with the competition left back at the finish line, the victor trots victoriously around the track. All the TV cameras and every eye from the "cloud of witnesses" are fixed upon the winner. Praises ring loud at the winner's great accomplishment.

In a sense whenever we run as a Christian, we are running a victory lap because Christ has won the victory for us over sin and death. However, God has provided another type of "victory lap" for His people and for Himself that we'll see in the next chapter.

As we have seen in Revelation 10: 1-11, John sees a mighty angel who has his right foot upon the sea and his left foot upon the earth. This angel has a "little book" opened in his hand. John is instructed to go and take the little book out of the angel's hand and to eat it. I believe it was this Book of Revelation because the angel told him, *"Thou must prophesy again before many peoples, and nations, and tongues, and kings."* (Verse 11) The book tasted sweet in John's mouth but was bitter in his belly. The Word of God is pleasant to the taste because it tells us about the blessedness and final victory for Christ and us. But it is bitter because we hold values that arouse the world's wrath and bring us persecution, suffering, and even death. And also because the Word declares the terrible trouble God will bring on those who reject its message.

The return of Christ is an event that those running the Christian race have awaited with great anticipation since our Lord ascended to the right hand of our Father. We are told in 1Thessalonians 4:13-17 that He *"shall descend from heaven with a shout, with the voice of the archangel, and with the trump of God: and the dead in Christ shall rise first: Then we which are alive and remain shall be caught up together with them in the air: and so shall we ever be with the Lord."* As we have seen, the Church – the visible kingdom of God – is removed before God's punishment and full wrath is poured out on the earth over the next seven years.

Then we saw the Lord's judgment of the saints at the Judgment Seat of Christ. Also, in Revelation 19:7, we rejoice because *"the marriage of the Lamb is come, and his wife hath made herself ready."* We then proceed to earth with the Lord leading us to the Battle of Armageddon to rule and reign with the Lord on the earth. This is just the beginning of the "victory lap" our Great God has prepared for His people.

Revelation 14:1-5

¹ Then I looked, and behold, a Lamb standing on Mount Zion, and with Him one hundred and forty-four thousand, having His Father's name written on their foreheads. ²And I heard a voice from heaven, like the voice of many waters, and like the voice of loud thunder. And I heard the sound of harpists playing their harps. ³They sang as it were a new song before the throne, before the four living creatures, and the elders; and no one could learn that song except the hundred and forty-four thousand who were redeemed from the earth. ⁴These are the ones who were not defiled with women, for they are virgins. These are the ones who follow the Lamb wherever He goes. These were redeemed from among men, being firstfruits to God and to the Lamb. ⁵And in their mouth was found no deceit, for they are without fault before the throne of God.

We who have returned with Christ, and those who have become the first fruits (i.e. the 144,000 believers) of His dealings with Israel during the period, as well as those resurrected believers, who were beheaded for Christ can now be seen preparing to rule and reign with Christ. The resurrection of those who were beheaded is known as *"the first resurrection."*

Revelation 20: 4-6

⁴And I saw thrones, and they sat on them, and judgment was committed to them. Then I saw the souls of those who had been beheaded for their witness to Jesus and for the word of God, who had not worshiped the beast or his image, and had not received his mark on their foreheads or on their hands. And they lived and reigned with Christ for a thousand years. ⁵But the rest of the dead did not live again until the thousand years were finished. This is the first resurrection. ⁶Blessed and holy is he who has part in the first resurrection. Over such the second death has no power, but they shall be priests of God and of Christ, and shall reign with Him a thousand years.

Since the Garden of Eden, our Father has pursued a heart-felt, sincere and loving relationship with man, who was created in His own image to fellowship with God. He sent Christ to live before us and show us what He, Himself, is like – to call us no longer servants but friends! He also gave Christ to be the Perfect Sacrifice – once and for all time – for the sins of the world. Our Father was pleased with this sacrifice, and the separation between He and man was bridged by the cross of Christ. All who accept this sacrifice for their sins (i.e. *"call upon the name of the Lord" Romans 10: 13*) shall be saved and become a child of God. As Christ resurrected from the grave to new life, so the child of God receives new life in Him. 1 Corinthians 1:30. And now, we have just seen that all His followers (i.e. those raptured, those who die for Him during the Tribulation, and those redeemed of Israel during the Tribulation) will rule and reign with Christ on earth for 1000 years.

During this reign, the earth is replenished after millions lose their lives through the wrath of God and the Battle of Armageddon. The lifetime of man is prolonged so that the gospel message is passed on to many generations throughout the 1000 years. Men and women, boys and girls are able to meet Christ personally and see Him face to face during His reign on earth. And very much like those who visited Solomon to hear his wisdom, many will travel thousands of miles to see and speak with Christ – to see His scars from the crucifixion – and have Him expound the Word of God to them. Their hearts will burn within them as they listen to Him and later when they share this experience with loved ones.

As unbelievable as it may seem, however, there will be those who resist Christ's love. They will want to be ruler of their own lives – rather than Christ. They want to assert their own character qualities and priorities rather than the Lord's values. They have the spirit of Nimrod rather than the Spirit of Christ. To separate the "wheat from the tares" (i.e. His people from His enemies), the Lord releases Satan from his chains. He deceives millions and mounts a campaign to attack Christ in Jerusalem. God wastes no time with this rebellion and sends fire to extinguish them immediately. This final spiritual battle being ended, Satan is thrown into the Lake of Fire where the Antichrist and False Prophet are.

Revelation 20:7-10

[7]Now when the thousand years have expired, Satan will be released from his prison [8]and will go out to deceive the nations which are in the four corners of the earth, Gog and Magog, to gather them together to battle, whose number is as the sand of the sea. [9]They went up on the breadth of the earth and surrounded the camp of the saints and the beloved city. And fire came down from God out of heaven and devoured them. [10]The devil, who deceived them, was cast into the lake of fire and brimstone where the beast and the false prophet are. And they will be tormented day and night forever and ever.

MORE INFORMATION FROM SCRIPTURE

> *Matthew 25: 31-46. "When the Son of man shall come in his glory, and all the holy angels with him, then shall he sit*

upon the throne of his glory: And before him shall be gathered all the nations: and he shall separate them one from another, as a shepherd divideth his sheep from the goats: And he shall set the sheep on his right hand, but the goats on the left. Then shall the King say unto them on his right hand, Come, ye blessed of my Father, inherit the kingdom prepared for you from the foundation of the world: For when I was an hungred, and ye gave me meat: I was thirsty and ye gave me drink: I was a stranger, and ye took me in: Naked and ye clothed me: I was sick and ye visited me: I was in prison, and ye came unto me. Then shall the righteous answer him saying, Lord, when saw we thee hungred, and fed thee? Or thirsty and gave thee drink? When saw we thee a stranger, and took thee in? or naked, and clothed thee? Or when saw we thee sick, or in prison, and came unto thee? And the King shall answer and say unto them, Verily I say unto you, Inasmuch as ye have done it unto the least of these my brethren, ye have done it unto me.

Then shall he say also unto them on the left hand, Depart from me, ye cursed, into everlasting fire, prepared for the devil and his angels: For I was an hungred, and ye gave me no meat: I was thirsty and ye gave me no drink: I was a stranger, and ye took me not in; naked, and ye clothed me not: sick, and in prison, and ye visited me not. Then shall they also answer him saying, Lord, when saw we thee an hungred, or athirst, or a stranger, or naked, or sick, or in prison, and did not minister unto thee? Then shall he answer them, saying, Verily I say unto you, Inasmuch as ye did it not to one of the least of these, ye did it not unto me. And these shall go away into everlasting punishment; but the righteous into life eternal."

HERE'S WHAT SCRIPTURE SAYS ABOUT THE 1000-YEAR REIGN OF CHRIST ON EARTH…

- Jeremiah 23:5 – **Christ shall be King.** *"'The days are coming,' declares the LORD, 'when I will raise up to David a righteous Branch, a King who will reign wisely and do what is just and right in the land.'"*
- Isaiah 2: 1-3 - **Israel will be prominent.** *"This is what Isaiah son of Amoz saw concerning Judah and Jerusalem: In the last days the mountain of the Lord's temple will be established as chief among the mountains; it will be raised above the hills, and all nations will stream to it. Many peoples will come and say, 'Come, let us go up to the mountain of the LORD, to the house of the God of Jacob. He will teach us his ways, so that we may walk in his paths.' The law will go out from Zion, the word of the LORD from Jerusalem."*

- His rule will reflect His character:
    - Isaiah 2: 4 – **Justice.** *"He will judge between the nations and will settle disputes for many peoples. They will beat their swords into plowshares and their spears into pruning hooks. Nation will not take up sword against nation, nor will they train for war anymore."*
    - Micah 4: 1-4 – **All prosper.** *"In the last days the mountain of the Lord's temple will be established as chief among the mountains; it will be raised above the hills, and peoples will stream to it. Many nations will come and say, "Come, let us go up to the mountain of the LORD, to the house of the God of Jacob. He will teach us his ways, so that we may walk in his paths." The law will go out from Zion, the word of the LORD from Jerusalem. He will judge between many peoples and will settle disputes for strong nations far and wide. They will beat*

their swords into plowshares and their spears into pruning hooks. Nation will not take up sword against nation, nor will they train for war anymore. Every man will sit under his own vine and under his own fig tree, and no one will make them afraid, for the LORD Almighty has spoken."
- Jeremiah 23: 5 – **Righteousness.** "'The days are coming,' declares the LORD, 'when I will raise up to David a righteous Branch, a King who will reign wisely and do what is just and right in the land.'"
- Zechariah 8: 4-5 – **Peace.** "This is what the LORD Almighty says: 'Once again men and women of ripe old age will sit in the streets of Jerusalem, each with cane in hand because of his age. The city streets will be filled with boys and girls playing there.'"
- Jeremiah 23: 4 – **People safe.** "'I will place shepherds over them who will tend them, and they will no longer be afraid or terrified, nor will any be missing,' declares the LORD.'"

- The natural world is transformed…
  - Isaiah 30: 23-26 - **Climate**. "He will also send you rain for the seed you sow in the ground, and the food that comes from the land will be rich and plentiful. In that day your cattle will graze in broad meadows. The oxen and donkeys that work the soil will eat fodder and mash, spread out with fork and shovel. In the day of great slaughter, when the towers fall, streams of water will flow on every high mountain and every lofty hill. The moon will shine like the sun, and the sunlight will be seven times brighter, like the light of seven full days, when the LORD

binds up the bruises of his people and heals the wounds he inflicted."
- Isaiah 11: 6-8 – **Animals tame.** *"The wolf will live with the lamb, the leopard will lie down with the goat, the calf and the lion and the yearling together; and a little child will lead them. The cow will feed with the bear, their young will lie down together, and the lion will eat straw like the ox. The infant will play near the hole of the cobra, and the young child put his hand into the viper's nest."*
- Ezekiel 47: 9-10 – **Great fishing.** *"Swarms of living creatures will live wherever the river flows. There will be large numbers of fish, because this water flows there and makes the salt water fresh; so where the river flows everything will live. Fishermen will stand along the shore; from En Gedi to En Eglaim there will be places for spreading nets. The fish will be of many kinds--like the fish of the Great Sea."*
- Isaiah 65: 19-20, 22 – **Life is lengthened.** *"I will rejoice over Jerusalem and take delight in my people; the sound of weeping and of crying will be heard in it no more.* "Never again will there be in it an infant who lives but a few days, or an old man who does not live out his years; he who dies at a hundred will be thought a mere youth; he who fails to reach a hundred will be considered accursed. No longer will they build houses and others live in them, or plant and others eat. For as the days of a tree, so will be the days of my people; my chosen ones will long enjoy the works of their hands."

- - Ezekiel 47: 12 – **Trees provide food and medicine.** *"Fruit trees of all kinds will grow on both banks of the river. Their leaves will not wither, nor will their fruit fail. Every month they will bear, because the water from the sanctuary flows to them. Their fruit will serve for food and their leaves for healing."*

- Malachi 1: 11- **God will be worshipped and Christ's name known in all the world.** *"My name will be great among the nations, from the rising to the setting of the sun. In every place incense and pure offerings will be brought to my name, because my name will be great among the nations," says the LORD Almighty."*

- Zechariah 14: 16 - **Representatives come to see Him in Jerusalem.** *"Then the survivors from all the nations that have attacked Jerusalem will go up year after year to worship the King, the LORD Almighty, and to celebrate the Feast of Tabernacles."*

God's thoughts are above human knowledge -
He moves in mysterious ways
To work out eternity's purpose
Through time's short procession of days.
  - *Stiefel*

CHAPTER 15
NEW HEAVEN, NEW EARTH, AND NEW JERUSALEM

After the thousand years are over, the real "victory lap" for the believer begins. It's truly the fulfillment of the Apostle Paul's word to the Corinthian believers, *"No eye has seen, no ear has heard, no mind has conceived what God has prepared for those who love him."* 1Corinthians 2:9. The victory lap is called **"The New Jerusalem"**. It's the future home for all of God's people from where we will rule and reign with Him for eternity.

I like to call it "Honeymoon City" because God and we will dwell together and we shall see Him face to face forever. *"…the throne of God and of the Lamb shall be in it; and his servants shall serve him: And they shall see his face; and his name shall be in their foreheads. And there shall be no night there; and they need no candle, neither the light of the sun; for the Lord God giveth them light: and they shall reign for ever and ever."* (Revelation 22:3-5) It's "Honeymoon City" also because the angel who was showing it to John told him that this city was prepared *"as a bride adorned for her husband"* (Revelation 21:2).

My favorite name for it, however, is "Showcase City" because – like the winner of the race who runs the victory lap - God will have us on display for the whole universe to see the glorious and redemptive work of Christ. The crowds that once shouted for us to glorify "self" and follow the world, the flesh, and the devil, will be gone. In their place will be a "cloud of witnesses" throughout the universe who will constantly bask in the light of "Showcase City". They will shout the praises of God and His Christ as they are eternally reminded of God's awesome, magnificent victory!

How could a city be "adorned" to be a bride? And how could it be a showcase? Let's look at the New Jerusalem. The church is housed there – all the born-again believers from all time. They adorn its streets. We shall be shining like the stars in the firmament

(Daniel 12:3). The degree of radiance will be determined at the judgment seat of Christ as we have already mentioned. In a way, we'll be like the precious stones that form the foundation of the City (Revelation 21:19-21) - precious stones that have been cut and shaped in the "heat" of this wondrous race our Father, through Christ, has given us to run by the power of the Holy Spirit. The names of the twelve tribes of Israel, the descendants of our forerunners Abraham, Isaac, and Jacob, are inscribed at each of the twelve entrance gates (Revelation 21:12). And each of these gates were made of a ***single pearl*** (Revelation 21:21) – like *"the pearl of great price"* Jesus spoke of – which represents Christ Himself. The only way into the City is through Christ – the Entrance. *"…the kingdom of heaven is like unto a merchant man, seeking goodly pearls: Who, when he had found **one pearl** of great price, went and sold all that he had, and bought it."* (Matthew 13:45-46)

The foundations of the City have the names of the Lamb's twelve Apostles inscribed there (Revelation 21:14). And the streets are of purest gold like transparent glass (Revelation 21:21) – gold that Peter said was the precious faith of believers when it was tried with fire (1Peter 1: 7). Finally, this City has *"the glory of God. Her light was like a most precious stone, like a jasper stone, clear as crystal."* (Revelation 21:11) It was like a great glass case that contained the precious jewels of the Lord being displayed for the entire universe for ever and ever as a final victory lap of those who ran for their life God's way.

Some might ask, "Who in the universe will be there to see this great display – the Bride of the Lamb – the City of God's precious love?" Who will be cheering the Victor and victors? We know that the angels will be there, but who else? *"And the nations of those who are saved shall walk in its light, and the kings of the earth bring their glory and honor into it. Its gates shall not be shut at all by day (there shall be no night there). And they shall bring the glory and honor of the nations into it."* (Revelation 21:24-26) There will be surviving nations who did not fall for the deceit of Satan after he was loosed from his thousand-year imprisonment!

These nations will be those we will *"rule and reign for ever and ever"*. Revelation 22: 5.

But as we have already said many do follow Satan. A massive destruction occurs of millions who follow Satan's deception. When he is loosed, he convinces a great army of people from the nations to come against Christ. At this point, Jesus would have ruled on earth for one thousand years from Jerusalem – a place Ezekiel calls THE LORD IS THERE (Ezekiel 48: 35). God wastes no time in handling this rebellion. There's a great whoosh of fire from heaven that devours them! Satan is cast into the Lake of Fire. And God conducts what is called the *"great white throne"* judgment of all unbelievers from the beginning of time (Revelation 20:11-15). Death and Hell are now thrown into the Lake of Fire. Two different sets of books are opened at this judgment – the books recording the works of men and women as well as the Book of Life that has the names of those who are born-again believers.

Why would God use the Book of Life – with the names of believers in it - if this judgment is for unbelievers? Many, it seems, will claim to be Christ's followers, who never ran the race of life God's way! *"And why call ye me, Lord, Lord, and do not the things which I say?"* (Luke 6:46) *"Not everyone that saith unto me Lord, Lord, shall enter into the kingdom of heaven; but he that doeth the will of my Father which is in heaven. Many will say to me in that day, 'Lord, Lord have we not prophesied in thy name? And in thy name have cast out devils? And in thy name done many wonderful works?' And then I will profess unto them, I never knew you: depart from me ye that work iniquity."* (Matthew 7:21-23). These masses are cast into the lake of fire, which is the eternal death (i.e. *"the second death"* Revelation 20: 6).

Revelation 20: 11-15

[11]Then I saw a great white throne and Him who sat on it, from whose face the earth and the heaven fled away. And there was found no place for them. [12]And I saw the dead, small and great, standing before God, and books were opened. And another book

was opened, which is the Book of Life. And the dead were judged according to their works, by the things which were written in the books. [13]The sea gave up the dead who were in it, and Death and Hades delivered up the dead who were in them. And they were judged, each one according to his works. [14]Then Death and Hades were cast into the lake of fire. This is the second death. [15]And anyone not found written in the Book of Life was cast into the lake of fire.

When we read the following passage about a "new earth", please understand this to be a renovated earth – like a makeover of an old house. One of the "alterations" is the elimination of any seas. People continue living there.

Revelation 21: 1-27

[1] Now I saw a new heaven and a new earth, for the first heaven and the first earth had passed away. Also there was no more sea. [2]Then I, John, saw the holy city, New Jerusalem, coming down out of heaven from God, prepared as a bride adorned for her husband. [3]And I heard a loud voice from heaven saying, "Behold, the tabernacle of God is with men, and He will dwell with them, and they shall be His people. God Himself will be with them and be their God. [4]And God will wipe away every tear from their eyes; there shall be no more death, nor sorrow, nor crying. There shall be no more pain, for the former things have passed away."

[5]Then He who sat on the throne said, "Behold, I make all things new." And He said to me, "Write, for these words are true and faithful."

[6]And He said to me, "It is done! I am the Alpha and the Omega, the Beginning and the End. I will give of the fountain of the water of life freely to him who thirsts. [7]He who overcomes shall inherit all things, and I will be his God and he shall be My son. [8]But the cowardly, unbelieving, abominable, murderers, sexually immoral,

sorcerers, idolaters, and all liars shall have their part in the lake which burns with fire and brimstone, which is the second death."

⁹Then one of the seven angels who had the seven bowls filled with the seven last plagues came to me and talked with me, saying, "Come, I will show you the bride, the Lamb's wife." ¹⁰And he carried me away in the Spirit to a great and high mountain, and showed me the great city, the holy Jerusalem, descending out of heaven from God, ¹¹having the glory of God. Her light was like a most precious stone, like a jasper stone, clear as crystal. ¹²Also she had a great and high wall with twelve gates, and twelve angels at the gates, and names written on them, which are the names of the twelve tribes of the children of Israel: ¹³three gates on the east, three gates on the north, three gates on the south, and three gates on the west.

¹⁴Now the wall of the city had twelve foundations, and on them were the names of the twelve apostles of the Lamb. ¹⁵And he who talked with me had a gold reed to measure the city, its gates, and its wall. ¹⁶The city is laid out as a square; its length is as great as its breadth. And he measured the city with the reed: twelve thousand furlongs. Its length, breadth, and height are equal. ¹⁷Then he measured its wall: one hundred and forty-four cubits, according to the measure of a man, that is, of an angel. ¹⁸The construction of its wall was of jasper; and the city was pure gold, like clear glass. ¹⁹The foundations of the wall of the city were adorned with all kinds of precious stones: the first foundation was jasper, the second sapphire, the third chalcedony, the fourth emerald, ²⁰the fifth sardonyx, the sixth sardius, the seventh chrysolite, the eighth beryl, the ninth topaz, the tenth chrysoprase, the eleventh jacinth, and the twelfth amethyst. ²¹The twelve gates were twelve pearls: each individual gate was of one pearl. And the street of the city was pure gold, like transparent glass.

²²But I saw no temple in it, for the Lord God Almighty and the Lamb are its temple. ²³The city had no need of the sun or of the moon to shine in it, for the glory of God illuminated it. The Lamb is its light. ²⁴And the nations of those who are saved shall walk in

its light, and the kings of the earth bring their glory and honor into it. ²⁵Its gates shall not be shut at all by day (there shall be no night there). ²⁶And they shall bring the glory and the honor of the nations into it. ²⁷But there shall by no means enter it anything that defiles, or causes an abomination or a lie, but only those who are written in the Lamb's Book of Life.

Life will proceed as God originally intended for His creation to live without the influence of sin. The city will be about 1400 miles high, long, and wide. That's about 14 "atmospheres" as we know them today (i.e. after 100 miles we're in outer space). The city will have a river flowing through its center, from top to bottom. It will come from the *"throne of God and of the Lamb."* And on either side of the river there will be the tree of life, which will bear twelve different fruits – a different one every month. The leaves of this tree *"were for the healing of the nations."* (Revelation 22:1-2) The leaves of the tree of life will "heal" the survivors of the disaster caused by Satan's last rebellion against Christ. God acted with great love when He sent Adam and Eve out of the garden so they could not eat of the tree of life – because they would have lived forever in sin – and us too! (Genesis 3:22) God killed an animal to provide clothing to cover the nakedness of Adam and Eve. He would provide the blood of the Lamb to cover our sins. In Revelation 22:13, Jesus says, *"I am the Alpha and Omega, the Beginning and the End, the First and the Last."*

In the New Jerusalem, the tree of life is eaten freely. People live as God intended from the beginning with no more curse from sin (Revelation 22:3). God's home is with men and He shall wipe away all tears from their eyes. There shall be no more death, nor sorrow, nor crying, nor shall there be any more pain. The former things will all pass away and God will make everything new. (Revelation 21: 4-5)

Revelation 22:1-5

¹ And he showed me a pure river of water of life, clear as crystal, proceeding from the throne of God and of the Lamb. ²In

the middle of its street, and on either side of the river, was the tree of life, which bore twelve fruits, each tree yielding its fruit every month. The leaves of the tree were for the healing of the nations. [3]And there shall be no more curse, but the throne of God and of the Lamb shall be in it, and His servants shall serve Him. [4]They shall see His face, and His name shall be on their foreheads. [5]There shall be no night there: They need no lamp nor light of the sun, for the Lord God gives them light. And they shall reign forever and ever.

God, give me the faith of a little child!
A faith that will look to Thee -
That never will falter and never fail,
But follow Thee trustingly.
- *Showerman*

CHAPTER 16
CHRIST'S FINAL WORD

"FORGETTING WHAT IS BEHIND AND STRAINING TOWARD WHAT IS AHEAD, I PRESS ON…"
Philippians 3: 13-14

As our years unfold, what will be the central theme of the book our lives will write? What will our friends, neighbors, workmates, schoolmates, and our brethren say about us when our pilgrimage on earth is done? More importantly, what will our Lord Jesus Christ say about us? As we ask ourselves these questions, recall Paul's words to the saints at Philippi: *"I consider everything a loss compared to the surpassing greatness of knowing Christ Jesus my Lord…that I may **gain** Christ…becoming like him in his death, and so, somehow, to attain to the resurrection of the dead…Not that I have already obtained all this…But one thing I do: Forgetting what is behind and straining toward what is ahead, I press toward the goal to win the prize…"* Philippians 3: 8 – 14. The Prize he spoke about was Christ – being like Christ! That means surrendering ourselves as living sacrifices to God (Romans 12: 1-2) so He can make us into servant-leaders, who are in the image of His Son.

All believers are simultaneously leaders and servants. We are commissioned by the Lord as disciple-makers (Matthew 28: 19-20) and as His ambassadors (2 Corinthians 5:20). We, therefore, have influence over many people with whom God sets us. At the same time, we are called to follow and serve as His minister-priests (Revelation 5:10). As God told Elijah to anoint Elisha (1 Kings 19:16, 19) to take his place, similarly He gave Jesus direction and authority to anoint every believer. As Elijah cast his mantle upon Elisha, so Christ casts the mantle of the Holy Spirit upon every believer. Just as Elisha, who wanted a double portion of Elijah's spirit, was required to keep his eyes upon Elijah, likewise we go in the power of the Holy Spirit, and we keep our minds stayed upon our great High-Priest, Servant Leader, who is the Lamb upon the throne. Since Today is the day of salvation, let's offer ourselves – without restraint – to being used in both the leader and servant roles – but especially as His servant to others!

The Great Fisher of Men leads us often into deep waters where only Christ's outstretched, nail-driven hands provide the strength to keep serving others. We learn that it was not the nails that held Christ to the cross, but rather His love for the Father and us. Through it all, He presses into us the servant-leader qualities of self-sacrifice, faithfulness, endurance, patience, and love. Listen to what Jesus says about learning to serve: *"Just as the Son of Man did not come to be served, but to serve, and to give His life a ransom for many."* Matthew 20:28. *"For who is greater, he who sits at the table, or he who serves? Is it not he who sits at the table? But I am among you as the One who serves."* Luke 22:27. *"If I then, your Lord and Teacher, have washed your feet, you also ought to wash one another's feet. For I have given you an example, that you should do as I have done to you."* John 13:14-15.

We are leader – pilgrims in the world wearing the mantle of the Holy Spirit. And as long as the natural man lives in us, he (the natural man) is being progressively reduced so that Christ might increase. While we serve others here, we are in training for a wondrous assignment He has prepared for us – to rule and reign with Him throughout eternity! As we have seen, the Book of Revelation tells us that the resurrected and raptured believers are dressed in glorious white robes (e.g. mantles) in heaven. We are told that after the rapture of the Church (1 Thessalonians 4: 14-17) – which could happen at any time now – at the Judgment Seat of Christ, we will receive crowns; also, that we will lay them at the feet of Christ. See 2 Corinthians 5:10 and Revelation 4: 10-11.

In place of these crowns, we will receive a mantle of light – Mount of Transfiguration light – that we carry throughout eternity and *"shine as the brightness of the firmament…as stars for ever and ever."* Daniel 12:3. *"They (i.e. we) will see His face, and His name will be on their foreheads…They will not need the light of a *lamp or the light of the sun, for the Lord God will give them light. And they shall reign for ever and ever."* Revelation 22: 4-5. The name of Christ (i.e. "The Light of the World") will be on our foreheads!

As we've seen, one day we – with Elijah, Moses, Paul and all the other raptured believers – will return with Christ to defeat the Antichrist and the armies gathered at the Battle of Armageddon. Revelation 19: 11-16. We will follow the great Light of the World – the Sun of Righteousness. Together, we will look like His mantle of brilliant smaller stars flowing behind Him as every eye beholds the return of Christ. Then, as we have seen, what God told Abraham thousands of years earlier will be literally true: *"He (God) took him (Abraham) outside and said, 'Look up at the heavens and count the stars – if indeed you can count them.'* Then He said to him, *'So shall your offspring be.'"*

It's not surprising when you consider the life and ministry of Christ, as well as His warning to the seven churches, that His final word to us is **"Be ready!"** Don't just live for now. Live NOW with a view towards ETERNITY – a view given to us in this Revelation by our Lord Jesus Christ. Let's commit ourselves to press on for the Prize by being servant-leaders, priest-kings, who surrender as living offerings to the Master Sculptor's chisel – who remain steadfastly in the Potter's hand through life's trials - to be shaped in Christ's image for usefulness on earth and beyond. Serve others like the Master!

We could see Him eye-to-eye at any moment!

"I am coming quickly, and My reward is with Me to give to every one according to his work." Revelation 22:12, 20. *"The Spirit and the bride say, 'Come!' And let him who hears say, 'Come!' And let him who thirsts come. And whoever desires, let him take the water of life freely."* Revelation 22:17.

As we live our lives, let's remember the last recorded words of Christ in Revelation 22:20. They represent our Lord's last instructions, last invitation, last warning, and last promise: ***"Surely I am coming quickly."*** And John, speaking for all who are pressing toward the mark for the Prize of the high calling of God, adds the last prayer: *"Amen. Even so, come, Lord Jesus!"*

Revelation 22: 6-21

⁶Then he said to me, "These words are faithful and true." And the Lord God of the holy prophets sent His angel to show His servants the things which must shortly take place.

⁷"Behold, I am coming quickly! Blessed is he who keeps the words of the prophecy of this book."

⁸Now I, John, saw and heard these things. And when I heard and saw, I fell down to worship before the feet of the angel who showed me these things.

⁹Then he said to me, "See that you do not do that. For I am your fellow servant, and of your brethren the prophets, and of those who keep the words of this book. Worship God." ¹⁰And he said to me, "Do not seal the words of the prophecy of this book, for the time is at hand. ¹¹He who is unjust, let him be unjust still; he who is filthy, let him be filthy still; he who is righteous, let him be righteous still; he who is holy, let him be holy still."

¹²"And behold, I am coming quickly, and My reward is with Me, to give to every one according to his work. ¹³I am the Alpha and the Omega, the Beginning and the End, the First and the Last."

¹⁴Blessed are those who do His commandments, that they may have the right to the tree of life, and may enter through the gates into the city. ¹⁵But outside are dogs and sorcerers and sexually immoral and murderers and idolaters, and whoever loves and practices a lie.

¹⁶"I, Jesus, have sent My angel to testify to you these things in the churches. I am the Root and the Offspring of David, the Bright and Morning Star."

¹⁷And the Spirit and the bride say, "Come!" And let him who hears say, "Come!" And let him who thirsts come. Whoever desires, let him take the water of life freely.

¹⁸For I testify to everyone who hears the words of the prophecy of this book: If anyone adds to these things, God will add to him the plagues that are written in this book; ¹⁹and if anyone takes away from the words of the book of this prophecy, God shall take away his part from the Book of Life, from the holy city, and from the things which are written in this book.

²⁰He who testifies to these things says, "Surely I am coming quickly." Amen. Even so, come, Lord Jesus! ²¹The grace of our Lord Jesus Christ be with you all. Amen.

> Consider the blameless, observe the upright;
> there is a *future* for the man of peace.
> But all sinners will be destroyed;
> the *future* of the wicked will be cut off.
>
> The salvation of the righteous comes from the Lord;
> he is their stronghold in time of trouble.
> The Lord helps them and delivers them;
> he delivers them from the wicked and saves them,
> because they take refuge in him.
>
> - David, Psalm 37: 37-40

Sow a thought, and you reap an act;
Sow an act, and you reap a habit;
Sow a habit and you reap a character;
Sow a character, and you reap a destiny.
- *Anonymous*

EPILOGUE – WHAT THE WORLD COULD BE OR WILL BE IN 2030

Jesus will surely rescue us from an unimaginable future world through the Rapture of the Church. That great expectation, however, must not make us complacent about the things we see TODAY in the world and in the Church! Do you ever wonder what the world could be like for our children and grandchildren if the Lord delays His coming? What would it be like in 2030? Would you want them to live in that world? Here's a glimpse at what it could be like …

By 2030, man will implement a solution for the world's problems that's been planned in the computer age for at least 30 years – problems like providing low cost oil, adequate housing, ample food supplies, low cost medication, prosperity and freedom from wars for all. The only way that can ever work is for some person or group to be in charge of the world. The world authority would tell countries what they must share with other countries for solving these problems. Those rich in oil, food, medicines, etc. would supply others at a rate set by the world authority. Buying and selling as well as population, salaries, resources and the like would be regulated and recorded by using the computer technology. The easiest way to accomplish this would be by using a Universal Product Code and an imbedded chip in each person – on a part of the body that could be easily scanned. The chip would contain a unique identifier with information about residence, employment, special medical conditions, education, savings/checking accounts, and more. It would also provide Global Positioning System tracking of everybody. Kidnapping would become a thing of the past. Another by-product of this system would be no credit/debit cards or cash. The chip would perform these functions – so robbery would decline significantly. It would also eliminate most of the identity thefts so prevalent today. Most would be convinced that "life under a microscope" is a small price to pay – until the world authority traps them in a life of slavery to survive. Revelation 6: 5-6; 13: 17-18.

Today, many corporations are farming out jobs – manufacturing, technical, and service jobs – to countries that can do them at lowest cost. Some car manufacturing for the U.S. is done in Mexico. Computer-related work and customer service for phone companies is done in India. Other manufacturing is done in China. By 2030, very few job types could remain in the most prosperous countries where salaries are very high. Countries could be highly dependent upon each other for their prosperity. Technology would allow the world to become a global neighborhood, where various countries become our factories, storehouses, food markets, department stores, and home centers. Wealthy nations could be "deflated" to become like other countries so that a balance of economies and power could be created. This would at first appear to be the "best insurance for peace." But since the sinful nature of man – lust for power, position, and prestige – is not dealt with, all-out world war would be the end result.

Senseless murders – especially kids killing other kids and gang-mentality could cause the National Guard to be used as a police force in most countries. The need for conventional military forces will be reduced. Instead, "push-button" warfare will become prevalent. Though the world authority would attempt to keep countries from building impressive weapon systems, the advancing technology and new-found wealth of the formerly poor nations as well as distrust, pride, and lust for power could cause nations to build up anyway. China would become a formidable power. Revelation 16:12. Biological and chemical weapons as well as nuclear weapons and delivery systems would become easier for everyone to build and use. Ezekiel 38: 21-22. Revelation 9: 15-18.

Morality could continue to decay until there is no right or wrong. People would do whatever they considered morally correct in their own eyes. The vicious competition for viewers by the few international TV networks, the lack of parental concern, and the pressure for "freedom of speech", would cause unthinkable violence and immorality to sweep the world's airwaves. Lesbian and gay marriages could become as common as marriage between a man and woman. The campaign begun years ago to rid America of its Christian heritage, could result in an antichrist religion of "intolerance", which would then become the conservative American way. Family members could be in conflict with each other – children spying on their parents' unlawful Christian activity and turning them in to authorities. Matthew 24: 9-10. Men would continue to exploit women (and their increased wealth and "freedoms") in the areas of cosmetics, perfumes, clothing, and sex. Legal abortions and homosexuality could result in one male being available for seven females. Because of abortion, and man's selfish greed for material possessions, as well as his fanatical desire to create human life, "children-on-demand" could compete with natural child birth. These "convenience babies" could be raised by day-care networks around the world called "baby-farms". Most humans could be on some form of drug, which the world authority prescribes for maintaining world peace and happiness.

The church could be gone as we know it TODAY. It would be lukewarm at best. Revelation 3: 14-21. Years of Christians ambushing one another in the Church, along with unchecked iniquity, and complacency could result in coldness toward the things of Christ and toward one another. Matthew 24:12. The Lord would continue to be faithful, knocking at the door of people's hearts, and promising to be their Savior and Lord and to help them overcome this world, if only they would open themselves to Him. But most wouldn't. Missionaries from many other countries would try to reach Americans for Christ.

Is this the world we want for our children and grandchildren? If not, then we must act now! Luke 12: 34-37. Let's become "the Church the Bible built!" Put on the whole armor of God and stand against every evil! Ephesians 6: 13-18. Embrace Christ's character and priorities for yourself and your families. Philippians 2: 5-8. Emulate Christ in your daily behaviors at home, at work, and in church. Galatians 5: 22-26. To the degree that it depends

154 – What's In <u>Your</u> Future?

upon us, let's maintain the unity of the Spirit in the bond of peace – without compromising God's Word. Ephesians 4: 3. Let's wake up from life's routine, shake off complacency, and get involved in our churches, families, our children's schools, and our political and judicial systems. Be everything you can be for Christ so someday soon – when He does return – you will hear the words, "Well done, good, and faithful servant."

So what's in <u>your</u> future?

APPENDIX A

SUMMARY OF
WHAT'S IN <u>YOUR</u> FUTURE?

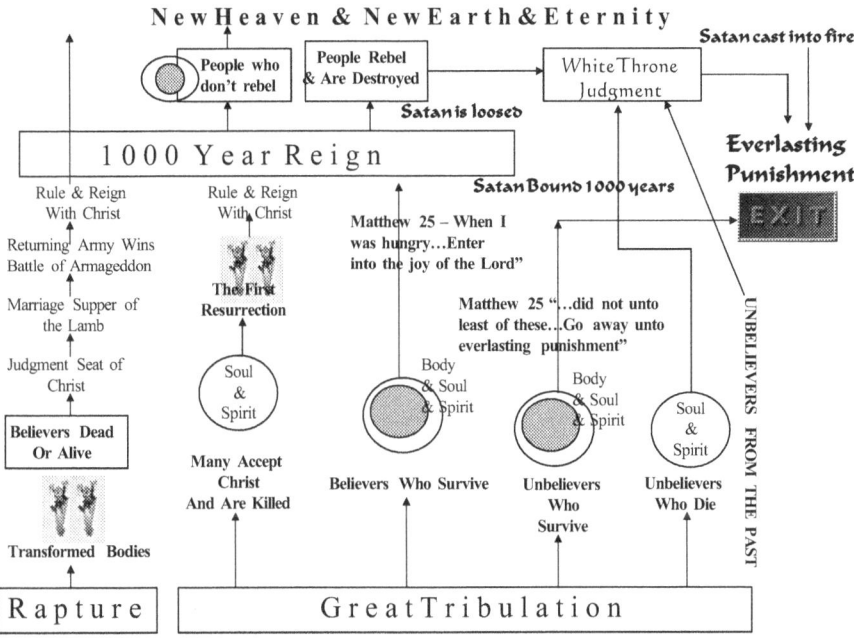

156 – What's In <u>Your</u> Future?

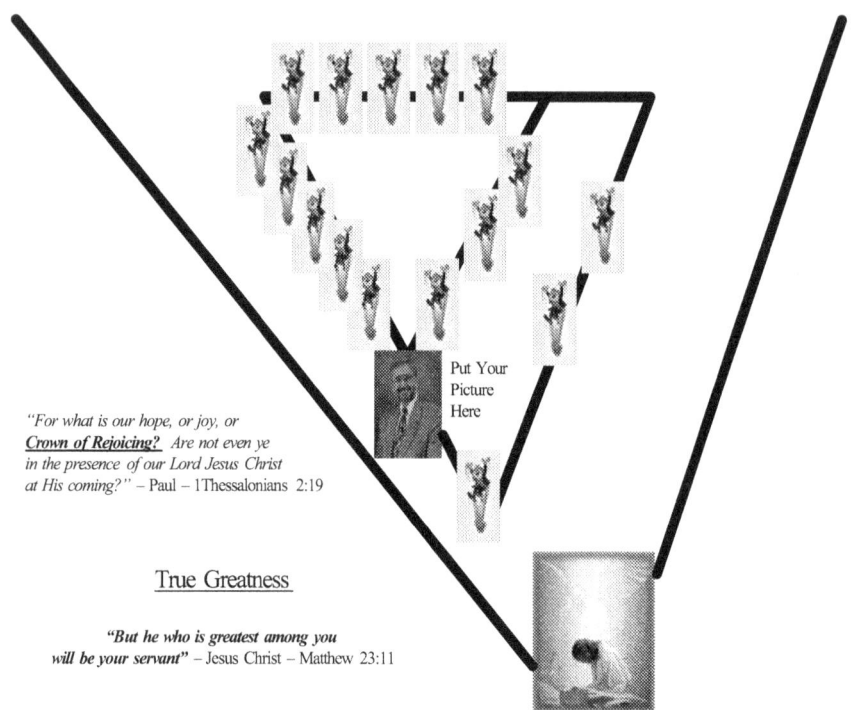

"For what is our hope, or joy, or <u>**Crown of Rejoicing?**</u> *Are not even ye in the presence of our Lord Jesus Christ at His coming?"* – Paul – 1Thessalonians 2:19

True Greatness

"But he who is greatest among you will be your servant" – Jesus Christ – Matthew 23:11

The Judgment Seat of Christ
Crown of Rejoicing

The Seven Churches of Revelation Summary Chart

THE 7 CHURCHES	1 Ephesus	2 Smyrna	3 Pergamos	4 Thyatira	5 Sardis	6 Philadelphia	7 Laodicea
SCRIPTURE REFERENCE	REV 2:1-7	REV 2:8-11	REV 2:12-17	REV 2:18-29	REV 3:1-6	REV 3:7-13	REV 3:14-22
MEANING OF NAME	"To Let Go"	"Anointing Oil"	"To Be Married To Power"	"To Be Ruled By A Woman"	"A Precious Stone"	"Brotherly Love"	"Power of The Laity"
PERIOD IN CHURCH HISTORY	A.D 96	A.D 100-313	A.D 313-606	A.D 606-1517	A.D 1517-1700	A.D 1700-1900	A.D 1900 - End of Age
CHARACTER OF EACH CHURCH	Effort Relaxed	Martyrdom & Tribulation	Union of Church and State	Counterfeit Anti-Christian	Reformation	Evangelical Missionary	Modernism Spiritual Poverty
CHRIST'S TITLE AS JUDGE	"Walks In Midst of Candlesticks"	"Which Was Dead And Is Alive"	"He Which Hath The Sharp Sword"	"The Son Of God"	"He That Hath The Seven Spirits"	"He That Is Holy And True"	"The Faithful Witness"
GOOD POINTS	Labor & Patience	Endured Tribulation	The Faith Not Denied	Fath & Patience	A Name That It Lived	Kept The Word	NONE
FAULTS	Left First Love	NONE	Balaam's Doctrine Idolatry	Ruled By Jezebel	But Dead Spiritually	NONE	Lukewarm
REWARD TO OVERCOMERS	"Paradise"	The First Resurrection	"A White Stone"	Reign With Christ	"Name Confessed"	"The New Jerusalem"	"With Christ On David's Throne"

Comparison of the Two Phases of Christ's Return

First – Rapture – Meeting in the Air

- Christ comes for His own
- Christians get imperishable bodies
- Christians taken to Father's house
- No judgment on earth at the Rapture
- Church taken to heaven
- Rapture could happen at any time
- Rapture will be a surprise
- For believers only
- Time of joy
- Before God's wrath on earth
- Satan's forces are occupied by Michael
- Christians judged by Christ
- Christians - Marriage Supper of the Lamb
- Only His own see Him
- Tribulation begins

Second – Christ Returns To Earth

- Christ comes back with His own
- No new bodies
- Resurrected Christians stay on earth
- Christ judges the nations (Mt 25)
- Christ establishes His kingdom on earth
- Seven years after the Rapture
- Signs for Christ's return (Mt 24:15-35)
- Affects the whole world
- Time of mourning
- After 7 years of God's wrath
- Satan is chained in the bottomless pit
- No judgment of Christians
- His bride returns with Christ
- Every eye shall see His return
- Christ's 1000-year reign begins

Characteristics of the Antichrist

Characteristic: Dan.9 Thes.2 Rev.13	(Coming Prince)	(Man of Sin)	(Beast from Sea)
Makes blasphemy in Temple	• X	• X	• X
Makes Idol	• X		• X
Demands Worship		• X	• X
Succeeds in Deceiving with Signs		• X	• X
Reign of Terror	• X		• X
Empowered by Satan		• X	• X
3½ Year Reign	• X		• X
Persecutes Saints	• X	• X	• X
World Rulership	(implied)	• X	• X
Destroyed by Christ at His coming	(Implied)	• X	• X

Source: Daniel's "Seventy Weeks", An Historical and Exegetical Analysis, Fred G. Zaspel ,1991.

Appendix A Illustrations -159

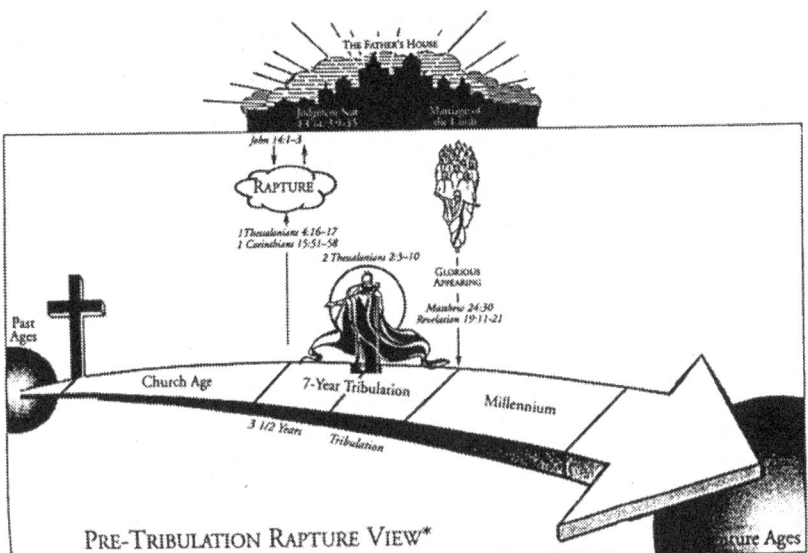

Seven Steps of Biblical Jewish Marriage

- **Covenant** – Bridegroom presents marriage contract. Spiritually, the Bride of Christ (i.e. the Church's) marriage contract was sealed in Christ's blood.
- **Cup** - If the price for the bride was acceptable, the couple would drink a cup of wine together. See Matthew 26: 27-28.
- **Price** – The more money paid, the more love was being shown and more influence on the father. Christ's price was the cross, bearing our sins, and rejection by man and His Father. See 2 Corinthians 5: 19-21.
- **Departure** – The groom goes to his father's house and builds a bridal chamber where the couple will "honeymoon" for 7 days. See John 14: 1-3. The bride stays "set apart" until he returns.
- **Return** – Only after his father approved the chamber could the groom return (Matthew 24: 36). The bride and her friends had only enough time to light their lamps and go. The groom and his friends would rush in, grab the girls, and make off with them (e.g. the Rapture 1 Thessalonians 4: 16-17).
- **Bridal Chamber** – After getting word that the marriage had been consummated, the groom's father started a 7-day celebration while the couple remained in the chamber. Jesus "consummates" His marriage at the Judgment Seat of Christ where He "takes away the Brides veil" and then "knows" all her spiritual secrets.
- **The Marriage Supper** – At the end of the week, the couple leaves the bridal chamber and celebrates a joyous meal with all the friends of his father.

So many gods have all come and gone,
God's of earth, of sky, and of sea;
But God the Creator alone will stand
Tests of time and eternity.
- *Carbaugh*

APPENDIX B

BABYLON AND CONTINUOUS SPIRITUAL WARFARE

1. SPIRITUAL WARFARE FROM ADAM TO CHRIST TO THE PRESENT
   a. GOD'S CREATION
   b. SATAN'S ATTACK - MAN'S FALL
   c. GOD'S SOLUTION – THE SEED OF A WOMAN
   d. SATAN'S ATTEMPT TO PREVENT THE REDEEMER SEED AND FRUSTRATE GOD'S PLAN
   e. GOD'S MOVE - NOAH AND THE FLOOD
   f. SATAN'S ATTEMPT TO PREVENT THE REDEEMER SEED - NIMROD AND BABYLON (IRAQ)
      i. NIMROD MEANS "REBEL". SCRIPTURE SAYS HE WAS A GREAT WARRIOR AND HUNTER (IN THE SENSE THAT HE REBELLED AGAINST GOD AND HUNTED MEN TO JOIN HIS REBELLION.
      ii. THE SOURCE OF ALL FALSE RELIGIONS
      iii. ONE WORLD DICTATORSHIP – HDQS IN THE CITY HE BUILT (BABEL)
      iv. ONE WORLD RELIGION – TOWER OF BABEL TO WORSHIP THE SUN (SOURCE OF LIFE)
         1. THE QUEEN OF HEAVEN AND HER "SEED" – SO-CALLED MIRACULOUS BIRTH OF TOMMUZ FROM NIMROD'S RAY OF SUN (HE BECAME PART OF THE SUN WHEN HE DIED)

2. THE COUNTERFEIT "RESURRECTION" – TOMMUZ KILLED BY WILD BOAR BUT AFTER 40 DAYS OF MOURNING BY NIMROD'S WIFE, TOMMUZ COMES TO LIFE AGAIN. AND HE NOT ONLY IS HER SON BUT ALSO HIS FATHER (I.E. COUNTERFEIT SON OF GOD WHO IS ONE WITH THE FATHER).
g. GOD'S COUNTERMEASURE – CONFUSE THEIR LANGUAGE
h. ALSO, ABRAHAM – TAKEN FROM NIMROD'S TERRITORY TO MAKE A SEPARATE PEOPLE, A NEW NATION – BECAUSE THE OTHERS WERE REBELLING AGAINST GOD AND TRUE WORSHIP.
i. ISAAC – THE FIRST DIVINELY CONCEIVED CHILD AND START OF THE NEW NATION.
j. JACOB (I.E. ISRAEL) & KING DAVID
k. GOD PROMISES TO PRESERVE HIS LINE OF KINGS
l. SATAN'S STRATEGY - LEADS ISRAEL INTO IDOLATRY WHICH LEADS TO CAPTIVITY & HEATHEN KINGS WHO RULE ISRAEL ("RULE OF THE NATIONS")
   i. BUT GOD DID PRESERVE THE LINE FROM DAVID TO MARY & JOSEPH & CHRIST

2. KINGDOMS – PAST, PRESENT, & FUTURE
   a. DANIEL'S INTERPRETATION OF NEBRUCHANEZZAR'S DREAM
      i. BABYLON RULES ISRAEL
      ii. MEDIA-PERSIA
      iii. GREECIAN
      iv. ROMAN

v. PART IRON, PART CLAY
  1. THE DIVINE STONE (CORNERSTONE – SMITTEN STONE, SMITING STONE) IN THE LAST DAYS
     a. ALL THE 5 KINGDOMS ARE PRESENT BECAUSE THE WHOLE COLLOSUS FALLS DOWN.
        i. IRAQ
        ii. IRAN (PERSIA)
        iii. SYRIA (ONE OF FOUR PARTS OF THE GRECIAN EMPIRE)
        iv. ROMAN EMPIRE COVERED MUCH OF THE WORLD
        v. PARTLY ISLAMIC & PARTLY NON-ISLAMIC GOV'T HEADED BY ANTICHRIST (LYBIA, ETHIOPIA, GERMANY, FRANCE, SAUDIA ARABIA, LEBANON, SYRIA, IRAN, IRAQ, ETC.) – POSSIBLY EZ 38 &39
     b. 6TH TRUMPET – "LOOSE THE 4 ANGELS IN THE RIVER EUPHATES" (I.E. IRAQ) TO KILL 1/3 OF MANKIND.
3. REV 17:1 "..THE JUDGMENT OF THE GREAT WHORE THAT SITS UPON MANY WATERS.."

a. WOMAN = FALSE RELIGION. "RELIGIOUS BABYLON". SHE'S DRESSED LIKE A PROSTITUTE WHO IS TRYING TO SOLICIT HERSELF TO MEN
   i. 17:5 "...UPON HER FOREHEAD WRITTEN, "MYSTERY BABYLON THE GREAT, THE MOTHER OF HARLOTS.." – GOES BACK TO NIMROD AND IRAQ – THE SOURCE OF POLITICAL DOMINATION & FALSE RELIGIONS

Two Babylons

Throughout the Word, God speaks of Babylon in two contexts – the physical place & the spiritual condition of man.

Physical Place
- The battleground - IRAQ
- The sin – Idolatry Re: Queen of heaven, Tammuz, worship of the sun. World domination by force under an antichrist type person
- The Beast – Nimrod, Nebuchadnezzar & later Sadaam Hussein
- The victims – All captured & killed by Babylon (incl. God's people Israel)
- The benefactors – Russia, France, Germany, Libya, Ethiopia, Iran, etc.
- God's judgment – Destruction by Medes-Persia and later by the U.S.

Spiritual Condition
The battleground - Man's heart
The sin – Everything that takes God's place through spiritual adultery (money, sex, drugs, education, family, friends, false religion, antichrist lordship)
The Beast – Satan
The victims – All people without Christ in their heart
The benefactors – Satan, Antichrist, False prophet, "kings & merchants" who lived "deliciously" through every evil practice
God's judgment – Salvation through Christ and the Gospel OR destruction by Christ

   ii. REV 17:9 "..SEVEN MOUNTAINS..SEVEN KINGS – 5 ARE FALLEN (EGYPT, ASSYRIA, BABYLON, PERSIA, GREECE)..ONE IS (ROME)..ONE IS NOT YET COME (ISLAMIC/NON-ISLAMIC REIGN UNDER ANTICHRIST).
   iii. THE BEAST (SATAN) IS THE 8TH
      1. JER 50 & 51 DEVOTED TO DESTRUCTION OF BABYLON

BY PERSIA AND BEYOND TO THE END OF THE AGE.

iv. REV 18:8-11. "POLITICAL BABYLON". KINGS OF THE EARTH WHO HAVE COMMITTED FORNICATION AND LIVE DELCIOUSLY WITH BABYLON LAMENT OVER HER DESTRUCTION. ALSO REV 18:20-21. REJOICE!

    i. TWO BABYLONS: PHYSICAL & SPIRITUAL

Create in me a clean heart, O God
Show the way that Jesus has trod;
Then I will tell of Your saving grace,
Until the day when I see Your face.
- *Hess*

TOPICAL INDEX

Angels of the churches   18
Antichrist   53-58, 158
Apostasy   39, 43
Appearance of Christ   13
Archangel Michael   39
Babylon   86-87, 111-116, 161-165
Battle for Righteousness   119
Battle of Armageddon   108, 116-117, 119-125
Battle of Ezekiel 38 and 39   120 – 121
Beast   54, 57-58
Biometrics   66-67
Cashless Society   60-61
Christ's character reflected   132-133
Christ's final word   145-149
Christ's names   5, 11-12
Christ's rule   127-135
Christ's Second Coming   41, 119-125, 157
Christ's sword   122
Chronology of events   7-10
Crown of Rejoicing   47, 156
Crowns of Scripture   50
Daniel's Seventy Weeks   99-102
Dragon   35
Electronic implants   64-65
Elijah   42
Enoch   42
Ephesus   19-20
Eye-to-eye with our Judge   45-46
Fatal wound   53
Final campaign for souls   77-81
Global Positioning System   63
Government military technology   63-64
Harvesting   78, 79, 90, 92-95
Honeymoon City   137
Inventory control and tracking   62

Jacob's trouble   80
Judge   11, 16
Judgment Seat of Christ   45-49, 156
Key that unlocks the Book of Revelation   77-78
Kingdom of God   16
Knowledge explosion   59
Laodicea   30-33
Lamp stands   18-19
Locusts   105-106
Messages to the churches   17-18
Mantle of Christ   119
Marriage Supper of the Lamb   73-76
Natural world transformed   133-134
Nebuchadnezzar's dream   54
New Jerusalem   137-143
New name   46, 147
Pergamum   21-24
Philadelphia   28-30
Prince of the Air   39
Rapture   39-43
Rededication to Christ   48
Remnant of Jews   35, 36, 92-93
Rise of the Antichrist and False Prophet   53-58
Ruling and reigning with Christ   127-135
Sardis   26-28
Satan cast to earth   35-37
Seals and Angel Messengers   83-97
Seven churches   15-33, 157
Seven heads   35, 53
Showcase City   137
Signs of Christ's return   40
Signs of the end of the age   40
Smart cards   64
Smyrna   20-21
Technology and the rise of the Antichrist   59-71
Three and one half years   36, 91
Thyatira   24-26
Thunder   73-74

Treaty with Israel   57
Trumpets and vials   99-118
Two witnesses   84-85, 91-92
Universal Product Code (UPC) Barcode   69-71
Unity of Christians   15
Victory lap for Christians   127, 137-143
What the world could become   151-154
Wilderness   36
Women with Crown of 12 Stars   35-36
World leadership today   55-56
Wrath of God   99-118

A Sunday school teacher, I don't know his name,
Was a wonderful person who never found fame;
Yet he shaped my whole life far more than he knew,
For his loving example has helped me be true.
- Anonymous

CROSS-REFERENCE INDEX

Revelation Chapter/Verses	Page Numbers
1:1 – 1:18	12, 13
1:7 (used twice)	121
1: 19-20	19
2: 1-7	20
2: 8-11	21
2: 12-17	23, 24
2: 18-29	25, 26
3: 1-6	28
3: 7-13	30
3: 14-22	32, 33
4: 1	42, 43
4: 2-3	49
4: 4	51
4: 5-11	74, 75
5: 1-14	79, 80
6: 1-2	83
6: 3-4	86
6: 5-6	87
6: 7-8	88
6: 9-11	90, 91
6: 12-17	94, 95
7: 1-8	93
7: 9-17	93, 94
8: 1-6	95, 96
8: 7	102
8: 8-9	103
8: 10-11	103
8: 12-13	104
9: 1-12	106, 107
9: 13-21	108, 109
10: 1-11	110, 111
11: 1-2	84
11: 3-6	85
11: 7-14	91, 92

172 – What's In <u>Your</u> Future?

11: 15-19	117
12: 1-17	36, 37
12:10-12 (used twice)	84
13: 1-5	55
13: 6-10	56
13: 11-17	57
13: 18	71
14: 1-5	128
14: 6-7	84
14: 8	87
14: 9-12	88
14: 13-14	89
14: 15-16	92
14: 17-20	95
15: 1-8	96
16: 1	97
16: 2	102
16: 3	103
16: 4-7	103
16: 8-9	104
16: 10-11	107
16: 12-16	109
16: 17-21	117, 118
17: 1-18	113, 114
18: 1-19	114, 115
18: 20-24	116
19: 1-3	118
19: 4-10	75, 76
19: 11-14	121
19: 15-21	122, 123
20: 1-3	123
20: 4-6	129
20: 7-10	130
20: 11-15	139
21: 1-27	140, 141
22: 1-5	142, 143
22: 6-21	148, 149

www.ingramcontent.com/pod-product-compliance
Lightning Source LLC
Chambersburg PA
CBHW051758040426
42446CB00007B/419